Everything about
PARISH
MINISTRY
I wish I had known

KATHY HENDRICKS

TWENTY
THIRD *23rd*
PUBLICATIONS
NEW LONDON, CT 06320
WWW.23RDPUBLICATIONS.COM

TWENTY-THIRD PUBLICATIONS
A Division of Bayard
One Montauk Avenue, Suite 200
New London, CT 06320
(860) 437-3012 or (800) 321-0411
www.23rdpublications.com

Library of Congress Cataloging-in-Publication Data
Hendricks, Kathy.
  Everything about parish ministry I wish I had known / Kathy Hendricks. — Rev. and updated.
    p. cm.
  ISBN 978-1-58595-199-4
1. Parishes. 2. Church work—Catholic Church. 3. Pastoral theology—Catholic Church. I. Title.
  BX1916.H46 2012
  253—dc23
                    2011052538

ISBN 978-1-58595-199-4
Printed in the U.S.A.

DEDICATION

To Eric and Anna,
who kept me grounded,

and

Ron,
who helped me soar

"*Everything About Parish Ministry I Wish I Had Known* is filled with real-life experiences and suggestions on how to work more effectively in a parish setting. An insightful read for anyone involved in ministry. We've been using this book in our ministry formation program for several years. It covers all the practical skills that are necessary for ministry. The author's experience makes this book come alive and is filled with excellent, wise, and useful tidbits which will engage the reader." Mary Fran Hartigan, M.A.,
Secretary for Catholic Life and Evangelization,
Director, Faith Formation, Diocese of Allentown

"I recommend *Everything About Parish Ministry I Wish I Had Known* for anyone ministering in a parish or thinking about parish ministry as a career. Kathy's writing reflects the insights gained from reflecting on years of ministry. Stories from her ministry give life to the book's practical advice. This book is like having a personal mentor. Like a good mentor, she asks probing questions, offers support when necessary, and identifies resources to strengthen your ministry. Kathy's use of case studies, examples, stories, checklists, and 'Your Thoughts' sections engage the reader in an adult formation style. The book is a reference book you will use often and a survey of the tasks, skills, and vision needed by the effective parish minister. A must-read for any parish minister." Donald R. Kurre,
Office of Religious Education,
Diocese of Grand Island

"How many times have we heard or even said ourselves, 'If I had only known...'? *Everything About Parish Ministry I Wish I Had Known* by Kathy Hendricks is a fabulous resource for anyone involved in parish ministry. Building on her over thirty years of ministry experience, Kathy shares a number of practical ideas and tools to help keep pastoral ministers focused, fresh, and renewed in their day-to-day work. It is a must-read for anyone involved in parish ministry, new or seasoned, and a great reference for those of us serving in a diocesan leadership. We will be adding this to our diocesan list of suggested resources for our parish ministers here in the Diocese of Saginaw." Paul Schroeder, Director,
Office for Evangelization and Catechesis,
Catholic Diocese of Saginaw

CONTENTS

"If you're going to err, err on the side of the pastoral"

Years ago I heard these words in a talk given by a bishop well known for his compassion, wisdom, and humor. He was referring to heavy-handed parish policies connected with sacramental preparation, ones that place unrealistic expectations upon young and uncertain parents. He called upon the group, mostly religious educators, to be warm and welcoming in their approach to ministry, relaxing their grip on policies and programs in order to be much more human and caring.

I could feel my face redden and my heart quicken. His message brought to mind painful reminders of the times when, as a parish minister, I was more concerned about rules than human needs. Looking back, I realize my actions often stemmed from being inexperienced and overly zealous. At times it was due to impatience, frustration, or uncertainty about the parameters of my position. My heart was generally in the right place; my style just didn't always jibe with those good intentions.

My work in ministry stretches back over forty years. As a young college student, my first volunteer "job" was as a singer in a group

1

that played for Mass at the school's Newman Center. Despite our rather limited musical abilities, the experience brought with it many of the rewards of volunteerism—camaraderie with others, the satisfaction of "giving back" to the community, and a way to learn more about the liturgy.

This first ministerial position led, in time, to others—Catholic school teacher, missionary, pastoral associate, committee chairperson, parish catechetical leader, diocesan director, national catechetical consultant, author, speaker, spiritual director, retreat facilitator, and parish life coordinator (lay "pastor"). My personal life also unfolded and added new sensitivities to my pastoral work. I married and had children, moved to different parts of the country, returned to graduate school, and continued my own spiritual growth as both seeker and disciple.

My diocesan and national work brought me in touch over the years with hundreds of ministers across the country and overseas. It is heartening to witness their dedication and commitment. They work hard to plan and implement catechetical and youth ministry programs, liturgical services, and social outreach projects, while also tending to numerous administrative details.

At no time in my travels have I heard anyone complain about not having enough to do. If anything, pastoral ministers are caught in the same bind as many of their parishioners. The pace is too hectic and the support systems too insufficient. Some are trying to juggle the responsibilities of family life with their parish work. Others find themselves isolated by time and distance from their religious communities. Priests see their roles shifting dramatically as the clergy shortages require their presence in more than one parish. Pastors and parish life coordinators are trying to cope with increasingly complex issues in the parish system, from personnel needs to liability worries.

Parishioners are changing, too. Statistical data shows an increasing number of "mixed" marriages, making for home lives in which religious culture is diminishing. Surveys show that Catholics no longer feel the obligation to participate in the Church. Mass attendance is erratic, at best, and it is not uncommon to see people attending churches of varying denominations in order to get their spiritual, family, and personal needs met.

It's a frustrating, exciting, and challenging time to be a pastoral leader. The work requires lots of energy, enthusiasm, optimism and hope, as well as openness to the unexpected. I know...After ten years of work on the diocesan and national levels, I returned to parish ministry and served for three years as a pastoral associate and then as the parish life coordinator.

My decision was deliberate. I wanted to be close to the struggles and dreams of everyday Catholics, and there is no better place to do it than in a parish. I also believed that returning to ministry might be a way to *redeem* myself for past sins. I resolved to be a more caring, sensitive minister, ready to "err" on the side of the pastoral. I hope I succeeded.

As I became re-established in the routine of parish life, I found myself saying over and over, "I wish I had known this when I started." A book idea was born.

It comes out of years of work that include both heady success and dismal failure. Ideas have emerged from personal experience, a collection of cherished resources, and stories shared with pastoral ministers across the country.

If you are just starting out, as a volunteer or as part of a professional staff, this book will serve as a helpful resource, showing you how and when to avoid some of the most common pitfalls in the work. For those who are seasoned veterans, the material is likely to affirm your efforts and perhaps generate some fresh insights.

How to use this book

Each chapter starts with a scenario that could be taking place in a parish somewhere at any given time. Use these to reflect upon individually, or discuss them together as a staff, committee, or with a group of colleagues. Mine your own wisdom and link it, as needed, to your particular situation. At the back of the book is a list of resources that I have found helpful over the years. You will notice that the material is quite varied. That's because inspiration often comes from the most unusual places. Add your own resources to the list as you go, or share them together as a group.

The Afterword will provide a means for recording what your own experience has taught you. It will also offer a way to concretize a plan for learning more about pastoral work. Complete this individually, or pull together ideas from the group with which you are involved. Either way, take advantage of the opportunity to make this book your own.

Part of this process means going straight to the areas that are of greatest interest to you. While the chapters are arranged in a loose kind of order, it is not necessary to read them in succession. Skip around as needed.

The purpose of *Everything About Parish Ministry I Wish I Had Known* is to help pastoral ministers better carry out their work and keep themselves renewed and refreshed in the process. Each chapter is written with a threefold focus:

- ► Helping the parish minister develop better relationships with the parish at large. Specific chapters deal with this in greater detail, particularly "Planning" (Chapter 3), "The Parishioner" (Chapter 4), and "Conflict" (Chapter 9).

- ► Helping the parish minister develop better relationships with colleagues, coworkers, and volunteers. Specific chapters deal with this in greater detail, particularly "Collaboration" (Chapter 5), "Coworkers" (Chapter 6), "Volunteers" (Chapter 7), and "Communication" (Chapter 8).

- ► Helping the parish minister develop better ways to manage their work and tend to their own spiritual needs. Specific chapters deal with this in greater detail, particularly "Leadership

Styles" (Chapter 1), "Time Management" (Chapter 2), and "Care of the Minister's Soul" (Chapter 10).

In addition to writing a book that I wish I had been able to access thirty years ago, my hope was to also put together something that was fun to read. Whatever else we do as parish ministers, we need to be mindful that we are just one small part of a very large picture. A bit of levity can go a long way in helping to establish a healthy sense of perspective. As a matter of fact, you might want to start out by reading the book's concluding passage and the prayer of a very beloved and wise pastoral leader—Pope John XXIII.

A note on the re-publication of *Everything About Parish Ministry I Wish I Had Known*

It's been ten years since *Everything About Parish Ministry I Wish I Had Known* was first made available by Twenty-Third Publications. After it went out of print, I self-published copies due to continued interest in the book. Now, I am very pleased to introduce a "third edition." My deepest gratitude goes to Twenty-Third Publications for putting the book back into national circulation.

In the years since the first publication of this book, I have worked with Protestant ministers who express the same frustrations and raise many of the same questions about what they wish to know about ministry to their congregations. So, as the book goes into another printing, my hope is that it will be a help to all of us, Roman Catholic and Protestant, who are seeking ways to minister to people hungry for spiritual guidance, meaningful worship, formation in faith, and the call to Christian discipleship.

CHAPTER 1

Leadership styles

"I am who I am"

Scenario

The alarm jangled Sister Mary Alice awake. With a feeling of dread she reached over and turned it off. What was it, she asked herself, that made her feel so reluctant to get up this morning? It had been a long weekend at the parish, with the full slate of Masses, an evening social, and a Saturday morning finance meeting.

She used to find her schedule invigorating. As pastoral associate she had a wide variety of responsibilities that involved welcoming and initiating people into parish life. A great "people person," she enjoyed the role immensely. Her work included newcomer ministry, social outreach, and the catechumenate for both adults and children.

A few months ago, the pastor had been assigned additional duties in the chancery, leaving him less time than ever at the parish. He asked Sister Mary Alice to take over most of its day-to-day management. This meant supervising staff and overseeing the pastoral council, finance committee, and stewardship campaign. In order to manage, she had delegated some of the work she loved so dearly to others. Her days and evenings seemed saturated with details, and she was beginning to think she was getting too old to keep up with it all. Rolling over, she managed to lift herself wearily out of bed. "I hate Mondays," she muttered as she stumbled toward the bathroom.

Your thoughts

? Is Sister Mary Alice "too old" for the job?

? What is causing her feelings of dread and hatred of Monday mornings?

? What aspects of her current position don't seem to fit her well?

The story of Sister Mary Alice hits painfully close to home for anyone who has had a shift in job responsibilities that depletes them of prior energy and enthusiasm. In my most recent pastoral experience, I was asked to take on the role of interim parish life coordinator for a period of six months. That meant managing all of the day-to-day operations in the absence of a resident pastor. The tasks I had relished—initiating and coordinating ministries— were handed over to other people. My time was swallowed up by budgets, personnel issues, and keeping a major building project on track. Monday wasn't my favorite day either.

What's Your Style?

Are you a driver or a rider? An E, an I, a J, or a P? An achiever or an affiliator? A dreamer or a doer?

If you know exactly what I am talking about, chances are you have taken one of dozens of leadership, personality, or work-style preference tests. These are very helpful tools in naming preferred ways of working and relating to others. They don't necessarily solve anything, but they do shed considerable light on why we find our roles either worthwhile or frustrating.

I recently began gardening and, in the process, learned that three things are necessary: priming, planting, and pruning. Each contains some wonderful connections to church ministry.

1. Priming. Every gardening instruction I ever read emphasizes the need to first work the earth. This entails identifying soil type and supplementing it, as needed, with other materials. It also requires breaking it up to make it receptive for the seeds, bulbs, or plantings that it will support. This can be immensely satisfying because it requires a feel for what nutrients might be most needed. Depending on the consistency, it takes a bit of muscle to loosen and soften the soil enough for the planting process.

Some of us are primers. We love to lay the groundwork for ministry by feeling out the needs and interests of the people we serve. Primers are the ones who initiate new ideas at meetings, sometimes to the irritation of those who want to see their previous bright ideas brought to completion. They are classic "Ps" on the Myers-Briggs inventory, content to leave things open-ended and up to others to carry out. Nothing will frustrate a primer more than a job with too many details.

2. Planting. What can be more satisfying than seeing something one has tended burst into bloom? Planting requires patience and a trust in the process of growth. It also takes attention to where and how things are placed. If too close they'll crowd each other out and, as a result, growth will be stunted. If they're too far apart, weeds have a perfect entrée to sprout and conquer. The garden looks sparse, and watering is less effective. Different plants also require varying depths of soil so that they can take root and flourish.

Planting a garden also requires foresight. Choosing and developing a scheme that will blossom throughout the growing season is a challenge. It takes study and the knowledge that gardens grow lush only in time.

The planters in parish ministry work side by side with the primers. Unlike the figure in the Parable of the Sower (Matthew 13:3–9), they know that seeds cannot be strewn haphazardly. They are not discouraged when new ideas, programs, or ministries don't take root all at once. They don't equate success with numbers, nor do they see catchall approaches as effective. Planters are people who trust the process of conversion and are willing to stick around to watch their efforts flower. They are also people who need new challenges in order to stay stimulated and enthusiastic about their work.

3. Pruning. One of the most difficult parts of growing a garden is maintaining it. It is not enough to prime the soil and plant the seeds. A garden must be watered, weeded, and cut back. It needs fertilizing and mulching. It needs to be tended. Pruning is essential for the continued growth of flowers, vines, trees, and shrubs. It takes absolute trust to cut back a thriving piece of foliage. It also takes knowledge. Cutting a branch or stem in the wrong place or in the wrong way can be fatal to its growth.

There is an absolute need for pruners in pastoral ministry. They are in it for the long haul. These are the background people who relish tending to the myriad details that exist in parish work. Often "Js" on the Myers-Briggs formula, they find immense satisfaction in seeing things through to completion. The constant introduction of new plans and priorities is a frustration to them. They are often the ones who have the unpleasant but necessary task of keeping everyone else grounded. Whether it's being mindful of a too-small budget or an overstuffed calendar, they remind others of the need to cut back, to refocus, to stay connected with the Church's essential mission.

Divergent and convergent thinking

Another way to look at preferences is through the way we make decisions and solve problems. *Convergent* thinkers ask, "What should be done today?" while *divergent* thinkers ask, "What could be done today?" Each style has its strengths and its weaknesses. Divergers dream the dreams and create possibilities. Their "out-of-the-box" thinking lends fresh approaches to tired ideas. This is especially beneficial in parishes that have dug deep ruts in their planning territory. Divergers shake things up.

If divergent thinkers ran the world, however, not much would actually get done. This is where the convergers excel. Being detail-oriented, they take visions and make them into reality. Divergers may consider them plodding or stodgy. Nevertheless, when specific, on-time tasks (such as issuing paychecks) need doing, convergers can be counted on for their vigilance and consistency.

You can find an excellent description of convergent and divergent styles in Chapter 4 of *Time Management for Unmanageable People* by Ann McGee-Cooper (New York: Bantam Books, 1994).

Is this a fit?

Several years ago the National Association of Church Personnel Administrators (NACPA) conducted a study on job satisfaction. Among their findings was that those who felt most satisfied in their work also experienced a self-role congruence. In other words, they fit the job they were asked to do.

This is no earth-shaking revelation. Yet there are a lot of Sister Mary Alices out there. Like her, they often start out enjoying their work and finding their talents and abilities put to good use. As circumstances change—perhaps through parish growth, personal achievement and competency, new leadership, or shifting personnel—they become more dissatisfied with the roles they are expected to play.

Every job is going to entail aspects that are less desirable than others. When the balance of what we do is tipped toward our least favorite tasks, we are bound to be frustrated. The trick is to tip it back in the other direction.

In the book *Soar with Your Strengths* (Delacorte Press, 1992), Donald O. Clifton and Paula Nelson argue that current educational and business practices encourage people to operate out of their weaknesses rather than their strengths. The opposite should be true, they say. "Excellence can be achieved only by focusing on strengths and managing weaknesses." The theory behind this is simple:

► Find out what you do well and do more of it.

► Find out what you don't do well and do less of it.

When we operate out of our strengths, we learn quickly and perform well. We take pride in our accomplishments because they are fueled by some of our deepest interests and desires.

Operating out of our weaknesses, we can become obsessive and defensive about our performance. Despite repeated attempts at something, we just don't seem to "get" it and, as a result, we think about it constantly. Instead of relishing what we have done well, we worry about what we've done wrong. Come Monday morning we want to stay in bed.

In our earlier story, Sister Mary Alice found great satisfaction in working directly with the people. Her move away from ministry and into management resulted in frustration and fatigue. This mirrors my own experience as a parish life coordinator. At first I thought I'd be in greater touch with parishioners, but it turned out to be the reverse. The bulk of my time was devoted to administrative tasks. On top of that I was thrust into a role that put my weakest areas in the spotlight: dealing with figures and details. I lived in constant fear that something gigantic would fall through a very significant crack—and there would be no one to blame but me.

Coping strategies

None of us is going to be able to work out of our preferred styles at all times. Every job—and parish work is no exception—has elements that just have to be tolerated. The question is degree. When we find ourselves in a role that is incongruent with our style, changes need to be made. Anyone who wants to stay in this work for long needs to develop good coping strategies. Here are five useful ones:

1. Delegating. It took a while before I realized that I couldn't—or shouldn't—do everything myself. For every task I don't enjoy there is someone out there who revels in it. Handing off responsibility to coworkers and volunteers can be a liberating experience. This takes an honest assessment of one's own limitations and a careful determination of the person's ability, interest, and willingness to become more involved. Then we have to be ready to let go.

2. Communicating. Some of us approach parish ministry like a huge Lenten sacrifice. Rather than air our concerns over being given more than we can handle, we "offer it up" in some mistaken notion that if it hurts it must be holy. I have met far too many people who, when asked if they've discussed their situation with the bishop, pastor, DRE, business administrator or other supervisor, are quick to protest. Healthy ministers are ones who set boundaries, and who readily admit what they can and cannot do well. They recognize their work as most effective when there is congruence between their strengths and their roles.

3. Sloughing. This is a strategy easy to grasp and hard to put into practice. It means, in the words of Clifton and Nelson, to "stop putting yourself in situations where you consistently fail." There is more in Chapter 2 on how to say no, so if this is an issue, you might want to refer to it now.

4. Collaborating. There is a very good reason why Jesus called twelve apostles and not just one. Together we form church, and our most deeply held beliefs and practices are understood in a context of community. Many of us work, however, as if it all rests squarely on one set of shoulders—our own. Chapter 5 is devoted to collaboration and how it can best be put into practice. If done well, collaborative ministry enables us to put our areas of strength to good use.

The ideal pastoral team is the one that includes each of the letters in the Myers-Briggs alphabet and covers all of the work styles and personality preferences. There probably aren't too many of these in existence, however. What we can do is seek out potential collaborators who offset our own weaknesses with their strengths and who appreciate our ability to do the same for them.

5. Stretching. We need only turn to the Bible for accounts of unlikely people who were called into roles that neither fit their style nor capitalized on their strengths. One of the best examples is Moses, a man with a severe speech impediment, who was told to talk Pharaoh into liberating the entire Egyptian workforce. Talk about self-role incongruity! He warms to his position—as do so many others—with an ever-increasing grace. God can indeed do great things in any of us.

Soaring with our strengths can be a liability when we define them too narrowly or when we presume we cannot move in new directions. The most vibrant parish ministers are ones who aren't confined by their own styles. They know their limitations but are not crippled by them, and they don't shut themselves off to possibility. Instead, they find creative ways to use their gifts and abilities within the parish and in other aspects of their lives. They stretch themselves by remaining open to what they've never before tried and by constantly learning and observing, falling down and getting back up again.

The leader's dream

In her book *My Grandfather's Blessings* (Riverhead Books, 2000), Rachel Naomi Remen describes a childhood memory of learning the story of the Exodus from her grandfather, a Jewish rabbi. It disturbs her to hear that Moses, after all his work in leading people out of Egypt and around the desert, dies before setting foot in the Promised Land. It seems so unfair she cries. "Moses was a leader," her grandfather explains, "and a leader always has a different dream from others. A real leader has the same dream that God has."

For some of us the dream is in laying the groundwork and tilling the soil. For others it is guiding and directing the growth of the community. For still others it is maintaining the plan and keeping it on course. Sister Mary Alice, like many of us, will have to discern whether her current role is out of sync with her best abilities and gifts. She may adapt; she may move elsewhere. Either way, the most important thing is to keep her internal light from burning out.

No matter what our styles, our preferences, our real or our ideal situations, there is much work to be done. All hands are needed to tend the garden that is God's church.

CHAPTER 2

Time management

"If only I had more time"

Scenario

Stan emerged from the room feeling cleansed, renewed, and full of resolve. It was time for changes in his life, and he believed wholeheartedly that his recent experience was giving him the courage and inspiration to make them. He strode forth with an all-consuming desire to sort out, purge, and purify. The relief it brought was enormous. As he got into his car, he knew he had come to the right place. Stan had just attended his first time-management workshop.

Stan is a youth ministry coordinator, a job he has held for just two years even though it feels like twenty. He enjoys the kids immensely, but the demands on his time are extreme. In college, Stan wasn't super-organized, but he did manage to juggle his studies, off-campus job, and social activities pretty well. Now it feels like his life is out of control. His day planner overflows with backed-up "to-do" lists, his voice mailbox is always full, and he is seriously neglecting his relationship with Sarah, his fiancée. He knows he is over-committed but doesn't seem to know how to break the patterns. Finding the workshop was a true Godsend as it provided clear-cut guidelines for organizing and utilizing time efficiently and effectively. He knows his life is going to improve dramatically.

Six months later, while sorting through the mountain of mail on his desk, Stan's eye catches a brightly colored flier: "Ten Sure-Fire Ways to Make Better Use of Your Time." He picks up the phone and dials the toll-free number. "I'd like to place an order...."

Your thoughts

? What is your experience with time management workshops and resources?

? Can you relate to Stan's initial hopes and excitement? Why or why not?

? What do you want more time for? How have you tried finding it?

Lessons from a juggler

Several years ago, I was working as a national consultant for a religious publishing company and had the unique opportunity to collaborate with a professional juggler. Once a year, the company convened its sales representatives and regional consultants to share information about new products, offer professional training, and regenerate enthusiasm. At one of these gatherings, a small circus troupe was hired as a way to carry out the theme of the meeting. Each day, the performers taught the group a circus skill, followed by a presentation that incorporated the skill into its theme.

I was one of the presenters; my topic was time management. So I worked with the juggler. It was great fun and I gained a number of interesting insights in the process. The most important had to do with what it takes to be a juggler. I posed this question to my new friend as I prepared my presentation. He, in true juggling fashion, tossed it back to me. Several responses came to mind. Dexterity? Flexibility? Balance? Eye-hand coordination?

"No," the juggler responded to each of my guesses. "All of those things are, of course, important, but they can eventually be acquired. The one essential thing for being a juggler is the ability to forgive yourself."

"For what?" I asked.

"For dropping the balls."

Pastoral ministry is a juggling act of major proportions, one fraught with potential for ball-dropping. Here are ten reasons why this happens:

1. People. Any job that deals with people tends to be erratic. This is especially true in a parish where emphasis is on ministerial service. Trying to stay pastorally sensitive to different groups and individuals—volunteers, parents, committee members, kids—takes the ingenuity of the most skilled juggler. Priorities need constant realignment as pastoral leaders attempt to stay in tune with the ups, downs, and in-betweens of the people in their care.

2. Demands. People come with lots of needs. They want to be listened to when they have an idea or problem. They seek help in their desire to grow in faith. They long for inspiration, comfort, and assurance as they face life's difficulties and challenges. For pastoral ministers, it is a constant learning process that requires stretching in new and uncertain directions.

3. Expectations. It's not easy working for an institution that has its origins sunk deep into scriptural soil. "Now the whole group of those who believed were of one heart and soul..." (Acts 4:32). The image this raises is that of a community where everyone "gets along," where mundane matters like bill-paying and snow removal never need attention. The trouble is that most of us read the Acts of the Apostles selectively, conveniently skimming over the infighting and power plays that were also part of the early Church's formation. It is a gigantic let-down to run headlong into the fallible and flawed dimensions of parish life.

4. Multiplying responsibilities. As one's level of competency rises, so, too, does the workload. One pastoral leader puts it rather bluntly: "If you're good they'll kill you." The more others see what we do, the more they think we *can* do. As a result, very few pastoral ministers end up five years later with a job that looks much like it did when they started out. Clergy shortages have priests overseeing several parishes at once. Cutbacks double staff members' work. New ministries and changes in diocesan guidelines generate overnight programs and issues. Unfortunately, as new responsibilities are added, old ones are not taken away. What began as a full plate has now become an overstocked buffet.

5. Vague job descriptions. As responsibilities multiply, job titles get murkier, thus creating a catchall situation for the exhausted minister. Not sure where to direct a call? Try Joan, the new "Pastoral Formation and Evangelical Associate in Charge of Ministry Coordination."

6. Messiah complexes. High expectations, increased competencies, "promotions" to new levels of responsibility—all can lead to serious problems remembering who, exactly, God sent to redeem the world. No, it wasn't me; and no, God didn't make a mistake in sending Jesus instead!

7. Administration vs. ministry. In 1992, the National Pastoral Life Center conducted a survey called "New Parish Ministries: Laity and Religious on Parish Staffs." It showed how, as roles and responsibilities shift, the need for administrative work increases. In fact, the study revealed that 68.8% of pastoral ministers reported having administration and organization as part of their work. Few of us, however, expected our work to go in this direction, and even fewer might have taken the job had we known.

8. Inadequate resources. To my knowledge, the word "cheap" doesn't appear in the gospels once. Nevertheless, it appears to be one of the operative principles behind the running of many parishes. Lack of adequate resources—everything from office equipment to textbooks—can create a terrific burden for ministers. If most parishioners use email, for example, but the parish office has outdated computers and no list of parishioners' email addresses, communication is inhibited. This doubles the time needed to send out simple messages. Having to scrounge for adequate and up-to-date resources is both time-consuming and disheartening.

9. Compulsions. Whether it's an inability to say no or thinking we have a personal responsibility for making each and every person happy, a compulsive drive for perfection leads to exhaustion and eventual burnout. Learning how to drop the balls may, in fact, be the single most difficult challenge a pastoral minister can face.

10. Incongruity between mission and reality. It's not uncommon to hear parish leaders bemoan the lack of attention they pay to their own spiritual lives while, in the same breath, urging others to "give more time to God." There is massive tension between what we know to be important and where we actually place our time.

Take these ten reasons for overload, and place them in Stan's mind as he furiously takes notes in his workshop. He is hearing all sorts of "rules" that will lighten his load and refocus his attention. Why then is he ordering a new book on the same subject just six months after his initial experience? It's because the rules don't work, or at least not completely.

In her book *Time Management for Unmanageable People*, Ann McGee-Cooper says that most systems today are outdated because they were written for "factory-based" time. This is time that was neatly blocked out for shift work, breaks, punching in and punching out. Tasks were easily defined because they remained the same day after day. She writes, "We take our current sense of time for granted, assuming that we think of time as people have always thought of it. But in fact the Industrial Revolution also brought with it a revolution in the way people in the West think of and respond to time. The growth of factories meant that people needed to be in place at particular times ready to join together in a single operation." Most of us, especially parish ministers, don't work that way. It's high time to take another look at the rules.

The Ten Commandments of time management (and how to break them)

"When you're racing with the clock...the second hand doesn't understand that your back may break and your fingers ache and your constitution isn't made of rock..."

— ADLER & ROSS, "THE PAJAMA GAME"

1. Be on time. I don't know anyone in parish ministry who has a single item to juggle. Instead, there seems to be a universal tendency toward feeling overwhelmed, of trying to keep one's head above water, of racing with the clock. "Falling behind" means time lost, wasted or misused. It means failure with a capital "F."

There are other ways to view time. McGee-Cooper identifies two that are particularly helpful:

▶ *Monochronic* refers to "time that is measured by the clock and typically decided in advance." Functioning in this kind of time, one is rewarded for being punctual, speedy, and brief. It's the fast-track view that is so predominant in modern culture.

▶ *Polychronic* refers to time that is relative and, thus, more complex. Functioning in this kind of time, one is rewarded for making intuitive decisions as events are playing themselves out, for being flexible, imaginative, and adaptive. Decisions are influenced not just by pragmatic matters but also by issues of trust, connecting with others, and how they will affect the quality of life. One way to determine your preferred style is to consider how you respond to the question, "So, what exactly do you do all day?" If you answer, "Well, *today* I..." you are definitely polychronic.

It's not hard to pick out the view preferred by most time management systems. The juggler image, very much a "polychronic" activity, isn't usually held up as an ideal practice. It is a good image for pastoral ministry, however, because the more one's work revolves around people, especially children, the more one is drawn into polychronic time. Ministers learn to respond to multiple needs, demands, and issues with the nimbleness and grace that make for first-rate juggling.

*"I think I have adult **Attention Deficit Disorder** but I've learned to call it 'multi-tasking.'"*

— DEBORAH BEATTIE, CORPORATE CONSULTANT

2. Do one thing at a time. Along with differing notions of time, we also work out of different styles of decision making and problem solving. In McGee-Cooper's words, "There are at least two ways to approach life, time, and work. One is the logical, practical, convergent way: define a task and get it done. The other is the innovative, intuitive, divergent way: define a task, then do something else."

During my work as a diocesan director of religious education, I spent a significant amount of time helping parish staffs resolve conflict. More often than not, the root problem seemed to lie squarely in this area—how people approach "life, time, and work"—and what happens when styles clash.

At a more benign level it surfaces in the way we view each other's workspaces. To give an example, my father was a classic converger—a place for everything and everything in its place. His desk was Exhibit A. File drawers were neatly arranged in alphabetical order; pencils and pens were kept in side-by-side compartments; cubbyholes contained miscellaneous items all sorted by common size or purpose. After his death, as my family convened to dismantle and dispense with his belongings, I found my two children standing in front of the desk, each of them captivated for a different reason. "That's awesome," my son exclaimed. My daughter stood beside him. Shaking her head slowly, she muttered, "That's sick."

Once again we find ourselves immersed in a culture with a definite proclivity for one style over the other. As McGee-Cooper says, "Society, business, and tradition tend to favor convergent [work] practices. Quick decision-making, sequential, step-by-step approaches, 'hard' data and facts, one answer rather than many—all are qualities celebrated by conventional society."

The good news for divergent thinkers is that, despite this commandment, juggling several tasks at once takes no more time than doing one thing before moving to another. In fact, it actually saves time because there is no need to constantly stop and nag oneself about finishing the job. It also sheds some brighter light on the next commandment.

"Creative clutter is better than tidy idleness."

— AUTHOR UNKNOWN

---

3. Clean up your desk. Why is it that some people thrive in cluttered environments, even though most time management systems advocate against it? Maybe it's because there are just two types of people in the world: the filers and the pilers.

"Pilers" remember things visually, not abstractly. They place things in "plain sight," sometimes using colors or symbols to help label them. Visual people also tend to be spatial. They put things down in spaces that make sense to them. That is how they can reach into a three-foot-high stack of papers and pull out exactly what they need.

Divergent thinkers often fall into this category. While juggling several projects at once, several piles are a necessity so attention can be shifted from one to the next. It's actually a time-saver because it isn't necessary to stop and rifle through a file drawer. Divergers also say the problem with a file is that, because they are open to so many options at any given moment, they often forget what name they've given it. Filing dooms it to extinction.

McGee-Cooper claims that tidiness is a waste of time for a right-brain person. Furthermore, she says if you can find something on your desk in less than three minutes, your system is working. If so, "God bless my messy desk" is a motto worth posting—assuming, of course, there's somewhere to put it.

"Never put off until tomorrow what you can do the day after tomorrow."   — MARK TWAIN

---

4. Finish one task before starting another. One request I made of the juggler was that he demonstrate how to manage irregular loads. Taking three items of different size and weight—a book, a pencil, and a tennis ball—he proceeded to juggle the whole mix with ease.

Achieving perfect balance may seem like the ideal way to work, but it is a rare occurrence. When a dozen different tasks pop up on our must-do list, it is overpowering. Our focus gets lost as we try to keep every ball, book, and pencil in the air. This is especially difficult for the convergent thinker who revels in sequential approaches to work. How does one manage?

Setting priorities is key; following the eighty/twenty rule can help. This means taking an entire day's tasks and choosing twenty percent of the items that are most important. These should receive eighty percent of one's energy and attention. The remaining eighty percent of the items then get twenty percent of the attention. Eighty/twenty prioritizing can be completed as part of a formal planning process or more simply by creating a mental picture of the day before getting out of bed in the morning. Picking out two or three things that need the greatest time and/or energy means setting other matters aside or giving them less concentrated effort. This relieves feelings of overload and helps make the day more manageable.

This system works well when life stays relatively stable. How do we respond when something unexpected is thrown our way? The experienced juggler catches it and works it into the mix. Some of us plan so tightly we have no room for unanticipated events or last-minute changes. Flexibility may not be written into our job descriptions, but it is essential for anyone who wants to make it as far as Advent.

Collaborative ministry is another good reason for breaking this commandment. Sometimes we take a project as far as it can go and then need to pass it to someone else. For those who love closure, this is a frustrating practice. It can also be an exciting one. Brainstorming, merging ideas, independent and group work, retuning and refining—these are all collaborative activities. The end result, if we're able to trust others with their share of the work, can be immensely rewarding precisely because it is a back-and-forth, give-and-take, throw-it-into-the-mix endeavor.

"Our two greatest problems are gravity and paper work. We can lick gravity but sometimes the paper work is over-whelming." — DR. WERNHER VON BRAUN

---

5. Handle each piece of paper just once. Three valid reasons for breaking this commandment:

▶ When I'm not the only one responsible for making a decision.

▶ When I need to gather additional information, input, advice, reactions, or directives before taking further action.

▶ When I need to give the matter more thought and reflection.

With the advent of "paperless" communications, the messy desk is now being replaced by the overstuffed inbox. Email serves as a substitute for the piles of paper that threaten to bury us in details. The two co-exist when we have a penchant for running off those emails. Either way, it's not always a wise idea to handle each one once, yet how do we manage the information overload?

The late Erma Bombeck once wrote a great "recipe" for making garbage. Take some leftovers, place them in a container, and put it on the refrigerator shelf. As more containers are added, the original one gets shoved to the back. As this process is repeated, the original one eventually makes its way back to the front. Open it up and voilà—instant garbage!

It's the same with paperwork. Label a file folder—manila or computer-generated—with some vague term like "For Further Consideration," and use it to stash paper and email that warrants neither immediate attention nor a first-class trip to the trash. Every week or two go through the file, which by now has swollen to the size of a World Book Encyclopedia. Sort through the items and it's probable that half of them can now be discarded because they've expired or become obsolete. Voilà—instant garbage!

"If at first you don't succeed, try, try again. Then quit. There's no use being a damn fool about it." — W.C. FIELDS

6. Make a plan and stick to it. In Chapter 1, we looked at the way convergent and divergent thinkers approach the planning process. Once again it's easy to spot the bias in time management systems for the converger's approach: sequential, scheduled, single-minded. Make a list and check it once. For a diverger, the to-do list is a continual source of frustration.

Because they are always opening the door to other options, their list keeps growing. No wonder their constant lament is not being able to get anything done. It's not so much about sticking to a plan; it's figuring out how to prioritize all those great ideas and options. (Note to the diverger: If you skipped commandment #4, as per your style, go back and read about the eighty/twenty rule.)

Have you ever procrastinated because something didn't "feel" right? At such times we are better able to juggle by holding back and giving the situation more time. This means letting go and moving to something else that needs our consideration. We may or may not return to the unfinished task, but forcing it into closure against our gut instincts would be the poorer option.

Letting ideas "incubate" may lead to a better plan. It's called "creative procrastination," and it rarely happens in an office setting. Going for a walk, daydreaming, and listening to music are some of my favorite ways of generating, refining, and realigning ideas. It brings me back time and again to the drawing board in which plans are purposely written in erasable ink.

"It's usually other people's clutter and junk that bother me. Mine always seems to have purpose and reason."

— ANN MCGEE-COOPER

---

7. Get rid of what you don't use. Whenever I set out to clear my office, I end up rearranging it instead. It reminds me of an observation my brother-in-law had about the attempts my sisters and

I make to have communal garage sales. "You ignore the customers, pore over family artifacts, and end up exchanging everything until the next garage sale." We listen and we laugh and we go on doing what we've always done. Our "stuff" has a history and, with enough ingenuity, we'll find some purpose for it, too.

My files are bulging with talks, notes, clippings, records, correspondence, and half-written articles. I know I should sift it out, but somehow I believe it all has some cosmic reason for being where it is. This conviction was affirmed when I recently found use for a comment I heard and scribbled down in 1993.

Nevertheless, I have to concede the validity of this commandment when it comes to time management. Having more stuff means having to be more organized—and that takes time. According to James Gleick, in his book *Faster: The Acceleration of Just About Everything* (New York: Pantheon Books, 1994), "Sociologists in several countries have found that increasing wealth and increasing education bring a sense of tension about time. We believe that we possess too little of it: that is a myth we now live by. What is true is that we are awash in things, in information, in news, in the old rubble and shiny new toys of our complex civilization, and—strange perhaps—stuff means speed."

We need to sort out for ourselves which possessions actually do have purpose. If the clutter is distorting our sense of time, it is a good idea to downsize. Schedule a day or an afternoon for this because, no doubt, it will turn into a lengthy and nostalgic process. Just try not to fall into the practice described by one DRE who told me, "I have no trouble getting rid of things. I just make a copy first."

"If we have learned the name of just one hormone, it is adrenaline."
                                                    — JAMES GLEICK

8. Technology will simplify your life. I once had a secretary who told me the phone was interrupting her work. She also asked for an enclosed office so she wouldn't have to be out in the reception area where all those people kept coming and going. Since part of her job was acting as a receptionist, this posed a bit of a problem.

As goofy as this sounds, she did have a point. Although answering phones and greeting visitors were part of her work, she also was responsible for typing reports, maintaining records, and cataloging resources. Being interrupted on and off throughout the day made these other tasks tedious and haphazard.

Since first writing this book, technological tools have multiplied rapidly. It's rare to find someone without a cell phone, and even rarer to see someone using it simply to make and receive calls. Social networks, iPads, text messaging, email, Skype...all of these devices and programs are keeping us plugged in to one another on a 24/7 basis. In addition, many of them are working their way into parish offices. They provide amazing benefits that allow for reaching parishioners, accessing resources, promoting programs, and creating networks across the globe.

They are also adding to the daily flow of interruptions, leaving one feeling at the end of the day as if nothing has been accomplished. As Gleick says, "For so many people and businesses, speed is connectivity. The state of being connected makes them feel more efficient—maybe even more nimble. Sadly, it also makes them feel busier—maybe even overloaded." Here are some suggestions for exercising some control over these tools so that they don't end up controlling us.

The *phone* can become a flexible servant rather than an insistent master:

▶ Schedule lengthy calls as if they were meetings. Call ahead to arrange a time, and prepare accordingly.

▶ Convert random calls to phone dates. Instead of rushing to get off the line because you don't have time to talk, schedule a more convenient time. This helps the caller feel valued instead of discounted.

► Practice being off-line. Let calls ring through to voice mail or a receptionist when working on something of higher priority.

► When reaching someone else's voice mail, try to eliminate the need for a callback. Leave a detailed message to set up a meeting, for example, and let the caller know you'll plan on it unless you hear otherwise.

► Practice cell phone courtesy. Turn it off or at least to silent mode when in a meeting or conversation. Ministry is essentially about presence. Having the potential for phone interruptions at any given time or place runs counter to the importance of giving others our full attention.

Email and the Internet can facilitate communication without contributing to burnout:

► Resist the urge to check and respond to email on command. It can be an incredible time-zapper. Block time as needed for this and then stick to it. Some time management experts recommend checking it only twice a day.

► Don't use email to vent feelings of anger, frustration, or annoyance. That "send" button operates instantaneously. Consider when the use of "snail mail" can be used as a "buffer," allowing you time to rework or reorganize a message, or to cancel it out altogether.

► Be mindful of the addictive potential of the Internet. While it is helpful to scour the web for resource ideas or take a break to play a computer game, it is possible to eat up huge chunks of time. More about this in Chapter 10.

> *"Don't let your mouth write a check your body can't cash."*
>
> — FLIP WILSON

9. Just say no. This is one commandment I don't advocate breaking. Sometimes we need to drop the balls on purpose. Doing so keeps us grounded. Saying no is part of this process.

People in monochronic jobs may be good at saying no when it comes to their own work because it allows them to operate in a more orderly way. They may resist hearing no from others, however. Take the example of a parish business administrator/bookkeeper. It's safe to say that, come payday, everyone appreciates this person's attentiveness to deadlines and procedures. When it comes to the more polychronic styles of others, however, they may not respond in a reciprocal manner. Why can't budgets be submitted by a certain date? What's the problem with keeping a time card? Why isn't everyone at his or her desk by 9:00 AM? Once again the potential for inter-office conflict due to clashing views of time festers and grows.

Just saying no to the demands, expectations, wishes, requests, and offers of others isn't easy. We have all sorts of reasons for saying yes, over and over again. These range from feeling nice-to-be-needed to a need to be nice. A new challenge may attract or a sense of duty hound us. Whatever the reason, here are some strategies for saying no:

- ► Block out the entire commitment on your calendar. Delay any answer until you actually see how it will affect your life.

- ► Get a second opinion. Consult with those who will be impacted by your answer: family, coworkers, and others.

- ► Rehearse saying no graciously, firmly, and thoughtfully. Take tips from people who do this well.

- ► Create a third right answer. Look for ways to share the responsibility rather than taking it all upon yourself.

► Examine your need to say yes. Is it about ego, guilt, or compulsions? If so, go back to rehearsing how to say no.

"Too much of a good thing can be wonderful." — MAE WEST

---

10. Don't waste time. What's harder to juggle—bowling balls or feathers? For jugglers, the throw is more important than the catch. Lofting a feather high into the air takes more determination than a bowling ball.

So it is with life. A lot of people are thrown into near crisis when their load lifts. Fear of being non-productive, of wasting time, of being perceived as apathetic or lazy all drive us into frenzied ways of working. It leads to the modern phenomenon of "hurry sicknesses," to which church workers are not immune. Even though we should know better (just take another look at the story of Martha and Mary), we are just as prone to falling into the "doing vs. being" mode as anyone else. Is this really what followers of Jesus should look like? Frazzled? Stressed-out? Anxious and agitated?

In a factory, regular breaks are scheduled into the day and announced with bells and whistles. This is not the case for the majority of workers today, including those in parish ministry. Lunch, if eaten at all, is consumed at one's desk. Night meetings and weekend programs lead to 60- and 80-hour workweeks. No wonder so many of us sense a loss of time.

In order to stay authentic, pastoral leaders simply must take time off for prayer and reflection, for strengthening relationships, for rest and relaxation. This means scheduling large chunks of time in one's calendar for retreat or recreation. It also means a daily practice of taking short bits of time for something refreshing, inspirational, and fun. Chapter 10 offers some ideas for doing this. Got time for a break right now?

A prayer for all time

Edward Hays wrote a beautiful prayer in thanksgiving for time in his classic book, *Prayers for the Domestic Church* (Easton, KS: Forest of Peace Publishing, Inc., 1979). In it, he reminds us that we stand in a "trinity of time—past, present, and future"—and that God is the source and sustainer of the time we have been given. It's a lovely reminder to befriend time and to stop often to thank the One who gifts us with it. When you find the load especially heavy and the balls crashing down around you, pause a moment to reflect on those thoughts. No doubt, you will find it to be time well spent.

CHAPTER 3

Planning

"Where is everybody?"

Scenario

Lydia arrives a bit breathless. She's later than planned and notices the speaker already waiting out front. Rushing up the sidewalk, she greets him and, together, they move inside. After getting him settled, Lydia quickly gets things in order for the evening—the welcome table, audiovisual equipment, handouts. A glitch arises when she discovers that the large coffee pot has already been taken, probably for the First Eucharist session taking place in the parish hall. "Oh, well," she shrugs, "people shouldn't bring drinks into the church anyway."

Lydia began as coordinator of adult faith formation just two months ago and is very excited about this, the first of three six-session Scripture series on the Bible planned for the coming year. It's been a lot of work, and she is glad that she was able to arrange for a professor at the local seminary to cover when tonight's original speaker cancelled. It was too late to announce the switch in the bulletin, but she figured it wouldn't make that much difference to those in attendance.

It's five minutes before starting time, and only four people have shown up. Lydia laughingly tells the presenter that, in this parish, people are notorious for arriving late. Fifteen minutes later a total of six people are scattered throughout the midsection of the church. One of them is the head of the pastoral council who apologetically tells her he can only stay for the first half hour since he has to attend another meeting.

After introducing the speaker, Lydia takes a seat in the back and ruminates about the low turnout. "I hope it's better next week," she thinks, as she watches the council chairman slip out the side door.

Your thoughts

? What clues can you find in this story that shed light on the program's poor attendance?

? What should Lydia do to prepare for next week?

? What is the most challenging aspect of parish planning?

Close to home

Several years ago, my first experience as a full-time director of religious education included a scenario similar to Lydia's. The U.S. bishops' pastoral letter on peace had just been released, and several members of the parish staff thought it made a perfect topic for a three-part Advent series. I was put in charge of the program, and work began. Tasks were divvied up; speakers were arranged; pulpit and bulletin announcements were made.

On the night of the first session, we planners arrived eager and excited. The speaker was in place, ready to share his insights and knowledge. We all waited...and waited. No one else showed up. It was embarrassing and infuriating. "After all of our work...," we complained to each other. At least we had sense enough to cancel the rest of the program and save ourselves further humiliation.

Looking back, I recognize several critical errors in our planning. First of all, we did not ask the parish if the series was of interest to them. Even a perfunctory glance at the membership would have given us a clue. A large population of retired military personnel was not likely to cram the pews for a presentation on the peace pastoral, at least not without some prior explanation of its content. Timing was also crucial. The themes of justice and peace were suitable for Advent, but not foremost in the minds of those caught up in the frenetic pace of pre-Christmas activities. Three weeks is a large commitment of time, and I don't recall informing anyone whether or not full attendance was a necessity for participation.

The ability to plan well is essential for all parish ministers. Good planning not only integrates and facilitates the work of the parish; it also makes our lives a whole lot saner. "Plan your work and work your plan," a supervisor used to tell me. A cliché, perhaps, but one that contains some practical wisdom. Let's look at this process and what it entails.

Find a focus

No homebuilder jumps into constructing a house without first having a blueprint. It works the same for pastoral ministry. Whether you are responsible for building a youth program or publishing the weekly bulletin, the need for a plan is vital. It starts with finding a focus. In Chapter 2, I noted that the juggling act gets trickier when coupled with vague job descriptions and poor prioritizing. Focus-finding is a case in point.

I served for six years as the director of religious education for the Diocese of Colorado Springs. Most of that time, I had the distinct pleasure of reporting to a supervisor named George who regularly affirmed and challenged my work. Each year, we took two weeks for my performance review, a process that included evaluating past goals and accomplishments, and putting together short- and long-term plans for the future. I remember the first time I proudly showed George my list for the upcoming year. To my surprise, he rejected it, telling me in no uncertain terms that ten priorities were way too much to manage. I had to redo them, narrowing my expectations of what could realistically be accomplished. It was a great, albeit humbling, lesson, one that taught me the value of doing fewer things well.

Tools for planning

In reworking my plan, I also came to appreciate two of the most useful tools at my disposal: the *calendar* and the *budget*.

The most common use of a calendar is to plan ahead. We use it to jot down appointments, schedule meetings, and highlight special events. It is a marvelous tool for keeping life's details in order.

Calendars can also be used for looking back. They should be reviewed periodically in order to provide clues as to why our plans succeeded or failed. The process can trigger some valuable insights. For example, a review of her personal calendar might have alerted Lydia to the fact that her Scripture series was surrounded by too many other commitments. She simply did not have the time to prepare in a way that would ensure the program's success. If she reviewed the parish calendar, she could see that, in addition to the First Eucharist session, there were other parish activities that drew participants away from her program.

Laying out one's work with the use of a calendar is like framing the house. It only contains the barest of essentials—the event or deadline itself. There is much more to do before the building starts to take shape. This is where a budget can help.

The creation of a budget is something worth investing a great deal of effort. The more detailed the budget, the more potential it holds for laying out a plan. Line items such as "food," "stipends," "advertising," or "books" are a reminder of critical details that are part of the planning process: hospitality, marketing, and resources. In conjunction with the calendar, the budget raises some essential questions:

▶ Who is the target audience for this event/activity?

▶ How will I promote it?

▶ Who else do I need to help with it—speakers, advisors, workers, cooks, musicians, etc.?

▶ What materials will I need—for the planners? the workers? the participants?

Whether or not I am responsible for actually creating an entire budget or just a piece of one doesn't matter. It can provide important stimuli to creating a blueprint for whatever house I am responsible for building.

"Just get it done is the motto carved on our shield of battle."

— CHARLES KEATING

The DOs and DON'Ts of planning

The "DOs"

Consult

Communicate

Pay attention

Let go

Be patient

In *The Leadership Book* (Mahwah, NJ: Paulist Press, 1994), author Charles Keating writes, "Planning...is like a road map that we refer to before we set out for a family vacation. The cost of ignoring it is to get lost." Lydia's bombed-out program, along with my own dismal experience, could very well be the result of naïveté and an overabundance of enthusiasm. In our eagerness to jump into implementation, we both short-circuited the planning process. The results speak for themselves. Here, then, are ten DOs and DON'Ts to keep in or out of the picture as we plan:

1. Do consult. As I will readily admit, the biggest cause for the failure of the long-ago Advent program was a lack of consultation with the parishioners themselves. No worthwhile planning resource is devoid of some recommendation for needs assessment. The problem with many of these, however, is that they don't contain the follow-up to the standard "what do you want?" question. This, quite simply, is: "Would you come?"

Let's face it—all of us are interested in a number of things we probably don't have the time to pursue. For example, every parish needs assessment I ever conducted turned up an interest in Bible study. When a program was planned and implemented, however, the Lydia-like attendance was demoralizing. Lots of Catholics know they should learn more about the Bible; whether they will actually do it is another matter. Consultation also must include coworkers, committees, and other parish organizations. Without it we plan on parallel tracks. This is counterproductive and diffuses everyone's efforts. The plan lacks integration and creates a competitive atmosphere, one that compromises the community-building mission of the Church.

2. Do communicate. "Perhaps the most important preparation...is lavish communication." These wise words from Max De Pree, in his book *Leadership Jazz* (New York: Dell Publishing, 1992), remind us that it is vital that we let others know, early in the planning process, what we are doing. Two-way communication promotes collaboration and innovation. It allows for feedback and ongoing evaluation. Done well, it saves time by eliminating the need for backtracking, apologizing, or damage control.

3. Do pay attention. In the 1980s, the National Advisory Committee on Adult Religious Education (NACARE) created an extensive planning tool called *Priming the Pump*. It placed needs assessment third on the list of planning essentials. The first was context. "Know your people," it advised. This may sound elementary, but it's surprising how many of us charge into planning without first taking parishioners into account. For example, it doesn't take much research to conclude that starting a nursery in a highly geriatric parish will produce few volunteers. Or that holding lots of weeknight events will lack appeal to families with school-age children. Demographics alone provide excellent insights into what will or will not succeed.

There are other factors that need attention in the process of planning. The use of advocates who critique and review plans from various perspectives is a great help. Over the years, I have consulted with individuals and convened committees who served as watchdogs for people with disabilities, families, women, youth, and ecumenical groups. Each one brought precious insights and inevitably drew me back to the drawing board time and again.

Just as valuable are skunks, those who serve as devil's advocates, critics, or pessimistic observers. Surrounding ourselves with cheerleaders may feel good, but their incessant applause drowns out other, more realistic voices. Some of the most important "skunk" messages I received over the years cautioned me about generational differences, challenged me to use real language vs. "churchese," and told me outright that my plan was lousy and what I could do to clean it up.

Using skunks doesn't mean opening ourselves to unrestrained criticism and unbridled hostility. It should not be an exercise in masochism. Chosen wisely, however, these straightforward people pull us up short and help us understand why our bright ideas are not likely to light up the neighborhood.

4. Do let go. My own family often provides the most valuable challenges to my plans. "Is this another one of your ideas that's going to bomb?" my son asked at dinner one night after I explained my newest plan for family "sharing." Yes, it stung a bit, but it also gave me a laugh and prodded me to take another look at how he had outgrown some of the activities I had in mind.

It can be a huge temptation for veteran ministers to keep dragging out the same old programs, newsletters, stories, or campaigns. All we have to do is fiddle with a few details, such as updating the name of the current pope, and we're all set. Have we asked ourselves if this idea has long since seen its glory days? Is it destined to "bomb" because our parishioners do not have the same interests, needs, longings, or time as the group for which it was originally designed?

There are some plans good enough to recycle from year to year. Like a good stock, they form the basis of a hearty stew. All plans, however, can use some spicing up, so that they look and sound refreshing and appealing.

5. Do be patient. "Nothing worthwhile in life is sudden." This memorable line, from Anthony Padovano's book *Dawn Without Darkness*, has been a mantra for my husband and me over the years. Whether applied to our marriage, our parenting, our dreams, or our schemes, its message remains refreshingly adaptive. Life is a process; good things take time to evolve and mature.

This is an important adage for parish ministry. If Lydia is completely disheartened by the initial reaction to her program, she might end up scrapping it altogether. That could be a big mistake, especially if it's a "first" in the parish. The scenario mentioned that she had been directing adult faith formation for only two months. Perhaps she is the first such coordinator ever, in which case it will take time for parishioners to know and understand her role and function. This can be true when overseeing a stewardship campaign, increasing participation at the Mass, training volunteers, or publishing a newsletter.

Innovation and experimentation tend to be messy. Our initial plans need to be constantly tweaked and tuned, reworked and rethought. This isn't just okay, it's wonderful! It means the plan is dynamic and the planner is aware that people-centered approaches tend to be roundabout rather than dead-on. Remember the definition of polychronic time in Chapter 2? This is what it's all about.

6. Don't over plan. Some us plan so tightly we have no room to turn around. The planning process resembles a row of dominoes and, as one piece falls, the others follow. I know of few instances where some type of follow-up—to an event, a meeting, or a mailing—isn't needed. If our plans are put together in a back-to-back fashion, we often have no time or space for this work. We then fall behind, and our plans seem fruitless and out-of-kilter.

The "DON'Ts"

Over plan

Entrench

Spin your wheels

Rationalize

Take things personally

Over planning can also lead to date-hogging. Each of us throws "our" dates on the parish calendar, oblivious to the plans of others. This is another downside of parallel planning; not only is it inconsiderate, but it is generally ineffective. Just ask Lydia. In Chapter 9 we will deal with sabotage and the conflict that results from this kind of planning. Cooperative planning, on the other hand, leads to the cherished win-win situations most of us prize. It may mean cutting back on our plans and whittling our priorities to a more manageable size. In the long run, this is a more productive planning method. If nothing else, it spares us the stress of sparring over space.

7. Don't entrench. At the time of the 1999 shootings at Columbine High School, I was working as a pastoral associate in Littleton, Colorado. The proximity of this violent episode hit our community like a sonic blast. Needless to say, all current plans were reassessed in light of this horrible tragedy. Our primary concern was reaching out to our frightened youth and their traumatized parents.

No parish exists in a vacuum. We are intentionally placed in the midst of cities and neighborhoods where life unfolds minute to minute. A factory lays off hundreds of workers. A new television series draws millions of viewers and becomes an overnight sensation. A suburb explodes with the influx of new families. A manically depressed father kills his young children and then himself. A drought threatens a farm community's crops and livestock. The local team wins the Super Bowl. Each event—large and small, profound and mundane—impacts us all in some way.

Max De Pree stresses in his book on leadership that institutions cannot afford to function in isolation from the rest of the world. It is essential to stay in touch with reality. The horrors and triumphs of life go on all around us. Effective pastoral ministers are attuned to the downs and ups that affect the people they serve. Good plans are thus written in pencil and are always subject to change.

8. Don't spin your wheels. "Writer's block" is a familiar term for most of us, and one that we might apply to some area of our lives at one time or another. Pastoral ministry is no exception. Perhaps we're hung up on ways to invite participants to small faith communities, how to add new members to the finance committee, or ideas for a catchy theme for a high school retreat. As any good writer will tell you, the best way to get "unstuck" is to move to something else for a while in order to refresh the mind and stimulate new outlooks. See which strategies in the sidebar on page 43 ring a bell with you.

9. Don't rationalize. Let's face it. Some plans do bomb. The worst thing we can do is deny it through glossy rationalizations such as, "Well, Jesus said where two or three are gathered..." Yes, this rings true for prayer, for faith-sharing, for intimate groups and activities. It does not work when a committee needs a certain number of people to make decision making reflective of the full community. Nor is it fair to either presenter or audience when an embarrassingly small number of people attend a gathering that was poorly planned.

Three ways to get unstuck

1 **Exercise your brain.** *Research has shown that creative blockages can be unplugged when using the brain in a different way. Work a crossword. Keep a book of brainteasers handy. Set up a puzzle and put a few pieces together at a time. Read a chapter of a mystery novel.*

2 **Vary your routine.** *Creatures of habit need to shake up their world from time to time in order to "see" things differently. Do your morning walk in the opposite direction. Eat dessert first. Take a catnap. Get dressed in a different order. Rearrange a drawer. Write your name upside down.*

3 **Try something different.** *Pastoral work can absorb so much of our time and energy that we curtail all other activities and interests. Try a new recipe. Plant a flower box. Read a different sort of book. Watch a new TV channel. Search the web for a learn-something-new site. Subscribe to a magazine unrelated to your job.*

I am a public speaker and, over the years, I have observed a number of things about program planning. Generally it's no surprise to me when I get to a parish and the attendance is sparse. These are the kind of indicators that have already doomed the program from the beginning:

"Just speak on whatever you want."

"This is for anyone in the parish who wants to attend."

"No, we don't need any information about you or your background."

"We realize it's Super Bowl Sunday, but are hoping people will get their priorities straight."

Sadly, this is the type of planning that often accompanies adult programs. Poor turnout is then blamed on the parishioners, who are accused of not having the "right" priorities.

Poor marketing and low expectations are two major problems in Catholic churches. Take a look at the average parish bulletin. You are likely to find some of the most boring copy in the world. Whether it is a program announcement or the sharing of parish information, there is a very good reason why much of it goes unread: dull, dull, dull.

For example, can you make sense of this bulletin announcement? Just for fun, circle all the words or terms that are likely to be foreign to the average parishioner:

— SAINT CATHERINE OF ALEXANDRA —
Parish Announcements for November 19–25

The PCL is holding an adult faith formation meeting for RCIA and PSR catechists to examine the GDC and CCC along with the OHWBWU document by the USCCB.   *RSVP ASAP. BYOB.*

By contrast, take a look at a community church—one of the many "mega churches" located around the country. Their facilities are often bustling with involvement. Why? They publicize brilliantly. They also expect people to take an active role in the community. Their "you won't want to miss this" approach outshines ones involving blackmail and guilt trips.

In our earlier scenario, Lydia would be well advised to shift gears at this point. Something didn't work and she needs to explore what it is before proceeding with session two. Even the most-well-thought-out ideas can end up being nonproductive. Good planning requires the honesty to admit when something hasn't worked and altering it as needed.

10. Don't take things personally. Do you think Lydia walked away from the church that night depressed or optimistic? If she's like those of us who want so desperately to do a good job, the answer is pretty clear. It's hard to step back from our hard work and view it dispassionately. Nevertheless, it is essential to do so. People respond or not according to their needs, not ours. Keeping this in mind can spare a lot of heartache.

Debriefing with other planners is an important aspect of evaluation. If the group is honest, it will be able to pick out what worked and why. A group can be more objective and work to refine and rejuvenate plans as needed.

How to do your job with fewer meetings

It's not realistic to put together a book on parish ministry without mentioning meetings. They are a "necessary evil" for many of us, zapping us of precious time and energy. Someone once defined a meeting as "the greatest illusion of progress ever invented." Planned well, however, they can bolster the work we do and strengthen our working relationships with others. Here are five steps to keep meetings manageable:

1. Be clear on its purpose. When planning a meeting, certain questions need to be asked:

> ► Why is it necessary and what is to be accomplished? Is it to inform, train, plan, make decisions, or dream? Who needs to be there and why?

> ► How much time will be needed? What is the most conducive environment for the work that needs doing?

> ► What are the anticipated results? The more we know about our purpose, the smoother the next four steps will fall into place.

2. Do your pre-work. There are all sorts of technological tools that can cover some of the work before a meeting takes place. In certain cases, it might do away with the need to meet altogether. Consider what consultation can happen first over the phone or through email or other online tools. What sort of preparation can participants complete that will cut down on unnecessary explanations and discussion? This might include background information, individual brainstorming, questionnaires, and, of course, reviewing the agenda. When each one comes prepared, things move along more effectively.

3. Create a usable agenda. Agendas outline the process and keep things on track by stating what we want to accomplish and within what time frame. In her book *Leadership Skills: Developing Volunteers for Organizational Success* (Tucson, AZ: Fisher Books, 1994), human resources consultant Emily Kittle Morrison recommends avoiding the following configurations when putting an agenda together:

▶ Two time-consuming items in a row;

▶ Two items of high emotion back-to-back;

▶ Two similar subjects, one after the other;

▶ Two routine items in a row.

4. Make use of a good facilitator. "Is anyone in charge here?" This question pops into our minds when a meeting rambles on with no apparent direction. A good facilitator follows the agenda and keeps the process moving. He or she may appoint others to the tasks of timekeeper or recorder and close the meeting by synthesizing key points and recommending follow-up. If facilitating is not your forte, find someone who can do it well. The results will be well worth it.

5. Follow through. Who wants to spend several hours at a meeting that never produces anything? When minutes are sent out, it lets participants know their involvement was noted. These notes should include significant accomplishments or decisions, particular follow-up actions or recommendations, and "next-step" information.

Burying the dead

Several years ago my husband and I moved to the city of Sitka in southeast Alaska. One of the first things I did was to get involved with the parish women's group. The members greeted me with great warmth and affection. After attending three meetings, I was elected president. I could say that my extraordinary leadership ability greatly impressed the other women. The truth was that I was new, I was young, and I was ignorant about the workings of the parish.

After my election I was informed about my first duty—organizing the annual Thanksgiving bingo and raffle. Assured that there would be plenty of help, I felt confident in my ability to do the job. As I started making phone calls, however, I noticed a definite slippage in participation. Most of the women were tired of the event, and there was no small amount of tension between them and the men's organization that traditionally set up the tables and chairs for the evening. Controversy arose over the women's decision to use the parish basement instead of the Moose Lodge, and the men went "on strike."

In the end, it fell to me, along with the good-natured pastor and my ever-generous husband, to get things ready. The event was well attended, and everyone seemed to have a good time. Even members of the men's group showed up. It was another learning experience.

There is no question that, as a newcomer, I had been taken advantage of. This position also yielded a vantage point from which I could raise a critical question: Why are we doing this? It seemed obvious to me that everyone was burnt out on the event. It no longer served any purpose for the community other than raising a few dollars. We agreed to bury it, and no one mourned its demise.

Some things in our parishes need to die. Like any death, there will come a sense of loss and possible resistance. My experience as a short-lived bingo chairperson taught me that burying outdated and joyless events, programs, and traditions often brings relief. It also brings the possibility of resurrection—new life that rises out of the dying.

I, for one, hope Lydia doesn't get discouraged, but finds some creative ways to rework her program. Planning is a mixed bag. It occasionally results in something brand new and other times in something ongoing. It frequently prods us to ask serious questions about what we are doing and why. Done well, it leads the parish forward and opens up new possibilities. Even token efforts are well worth the work and the time, the meetings and consultations, the cheerleaders and the skunks that emerge in the process.

CHAPTER 4

The parishioners

"Who are these people anyway?"

Scenario

Kevin hung up the phone feeling perplexed. He thought the weekend Masses had gone well. It was the first Sunday of Advent and the musicians made lovely selections, the lectors were expressive, and the homilies were mostly in sync with the season. As director for worship for the parish, he worked for months with liturgical and music ministers to educate them on the essential elements of Advent. Helpful information about the proper use of symbols and rituals was published in the bulletin and on the parish website throughout November. He knew that the Advent wreath was an optional add-on, and so the decision to eliminate it was liturgically sound. It took a while to convince the members of the worship commission about this, but eventually they agreed. Now he's just fielded three phone calls from people who reported the controversy brewing in the parish over this decision. How, he wonders, can it be that important?

Your thoughts

? Why did Kevin's decision create such a fuss?

? What bigger issues may underlie the elimination of an Advent wreath?

? What sort of decision might set off a similar controversy in your parish?

Several years ago I visited a parish in a small mountain town. Before entering the church, the pastor cautioned me about its overdone décor. One of his early predecessors, he explained, fancied himself a Michelangelo and covered both the walls and ceilings with elaborate paintings of religious scenes and characters. I was glad I had been forewarned. The little church was like a miniature Sistine Chapel. The major difference was the severe limitations of the artist. His lack of proportion resulted in elbows placed just above wrists and heads perched on unnaturally long necks. Palm trees and tropical flowers sprouted between scenes so that there was virtually no spot left untouched. Two life-size angel statues served up holy water near the vestibule. On top of this, no matter what direction they were facing, every figure had the exact same, distinctly patterned nose! The entire effect was one of being watched—carefully—by scores of mismatched eyes.

Later, I asked the pastor if he might ever broach the subject of an interior renovation. "No," he said. He went on to describe the pride the parishioners held for their church and the memories they cherished of the old pastor. As he spoke, I became aware of the affection he held for his people. He saw in their attachment to the paintings not a collective example of poor taste, but a deep and sincere connection with their past. I left feeling that I had come to know them a bit better myself.

Change is hard. In the Church, it can also be miraculous. Kevin ran face-first into this when he implemented his liturgically correct decision to remove an Advent wreath. What made sense on paper, however, didn't exactly jibe with the felt needs of the parishioners. While he had sound reasons behind his decision, he failed to consider the matters of heart, memory, and association that were deeply embedded in the community. Kevin did not know his parishioners the way the mountaintop pastor knew his.

It seems as if we constantly need to retune our headsets in order to really detect what our people need, want, and value. Keeping up with the times is an ongoing requisite in the life of a pastoral minister. It means letting go of assumptions and taking on the stance of an observer. The rate of change in our culture requires us to be frantic learners about who these people are, what they do, and what they care about.

It is said that some of the most powerful recruitment tools for religious vocations were the popular Fr. O'Malley films of the 1940s. Bing Crosby and Barry Fitzgerald, respectively, played the handsome young and the feisty but lovable priests. Throw in Ingrid Bergman as the stylish nun who could defy either man while still appearing deferential, and who wouldn't want to sign up? Their parishes and schools always had the right amount of tension— enough to keep things interesting but not enough to cause any serious burnout. Many are the times I longed for Fr. O'Malley's ability to croon away someone's sorrows or Sr. Bernadette's expertise in helping puny kids stand up to bullies with a few handy boxing lessons.

What makes films like these so appealing—and so unrealistic— is that they are almost always devoid of a real community. Instead, we see the needs of a few people and, as the credits start to roll, we rest easy, knowing that each of their situations has been neatly resolved. The crusty old benefactor will, in the end, save the school from demolition. The street urchin will turn into a cherubic but saucy choirboy. The wayward young woman will find true love while working as a parish housekeeper.

The genre out of which such films emerged was one in which Catholicism was seen as a separate subculture. It was one of our own making at a time when "keeping to ourselves" was considered a virtue. The outside world of "non-Catholic" behaviors, attitudes, practices, and beliefs was looked upon with suspicion, and the closer we kept to home, the better.

Since Vatican II, it is safe to say that this Catholic subculture has largely disappeared, at least in North America. The marvelous documents of Vatican II reiterating the role of the Church in the modern world truly did open windows and doors that had enclosed us for far too many centuries. Maybe it shed light on what was already taking place—i.e., that we could never really live in a purely "Catholic" environment, nor should we want to.

Given all of this, is it not realistic to think that there are—or should be—influences in the lives of parishioners other than the Church? We have only to read one of the many surveys about current attitudes and behaviors among Catholics and other religious groups to see that things have changed. The 2008 Pew Research Study is a case in point. It shows a dramatic shift in involvement in religious life among both Catholics and Protestants, including the startling statistic that "one-quarter of American adults (28%) have left the faith in which they were raised in favor of another religion—or no religion at all" (http://pewresearch.org/pubs/743/united-states-religion). Such studies include changes in the way Catholics and Protestants view moral authority, participation in worship, and what it means to belong to a religious congregation. We aren't talking "The Bells of St. Mary's" anymore.

What they do

When I first began writing this book, the television show *Survivor* was about to go into its fourth installment. As of this rewriting, it is poised to enter its twenty-third season! While the premise behind it—survival of the "fittest"—may be less than appealing to some of us, it is interesting to consider the cultural reaction the program has generated. Dozens of shows repeat the same "survivor" formula. Each acquires its own slew of contenders who are then eliminated, one by one, because they fail to lose weight, win the bachelor's heart, snag the modeling job, live up to idol status, or prove themselves as the most ruthless apprentice. "Survivor" celebrities from these shows make their way into movies, commercials, and talk shows. Parties take place around the airing of segments of the shows, and the final selection is often reported on morning-after news programs. It is ironic that a concept based on individual quests for survival has been transformed into a communal phenomenon.

Quiz

What do you know about pop culture? Take a few minutes to complete this "pop" quiz:

1. Name three television shows in the Nielsen top ten for the past week.

2. Name two books on the current bestseller list.

3. Name one of the top-grossing movies currently playing in theaters.

4. What team won the Super Bowl this year?

5. Name the current cover story for at least one popular magazine.

What is it that rivets the country to the rather boring spectacle of people trying to subsist on a day-to-day basis? It is, no doubt, tied to the thrill of adventure as well as to our continued fascination with Robinson Crusoe-type stories. It may also be linked to deeper issues of survival itself. While relatively few Americans contend with the most primitive requirements for shelter, clothing, and food, there is a huge struggle for survival taking place as anxiety over the economy ramps further upward. No wonder we turn to outrageous examples of people trying to outdo one another in order to stay on top and win the golden ring, no matter how tarnished and temporary it may be.

At the height of "Survivor-mania" we received a postcard in the mail. It was simply addressed to "our neighbors." On the front, a kangaroo posed against a backdrop of palm trees, jungle foliage, and craggy cliffs. A burning torch off to the side suggested a wild and untamed environment. A provocative question snatched the recipient's attention: "Who will survive?" The flip side contained a promotion for a three-part series at a nearby community church called "Surviving Life's Challenges." The session titles told the tale:

► "Family Survival Secrets"

► "Surviving a Stressful Life"

► "Marriage Survival Skills"

Someone at that church was paying attention to cultural interests and capitalized nicely on them. I can't imagine that this program bombed.

Maybe it came from trying to keep up with my own children as they grew or from my baby boomer experience as a lifelong TV and movie viewer, but I found pop culture to be an extremely helpful resource in my years of work as a pastoral minister. Keeping a close watch on Nielsen ratings, best-seller lists, and people's choice awards provided an interesting peek into what parishioners were watching, hearing, tweeting, posting, and prizing. I also met a fair share of colleagues who prided themselves on being culturally illiterate. "I never watch TV," they would sniff. The implied afterthought is that those that do are somewhere on the lower end of the spiritual fitness scale. Such attitudes seem not only snobbish but also shortsighted. There is a wealth of information to be mined in the perusal of pop culture

This isn't to say it is all healthy. There is a lot of narcissism published under the guise of "self-help" and a fair share of fluff passed off as "spirituality." What is interesting is the hunger that fuels the consumption of such material. What is it people are seeking? *Survivor*, for example, seems less about going solo than linking up with each other. In an impersonal society where identifying ourselves by PIN is becoming standard, is it any wonder that we want to know Oprah and Ellen on a first-name basis? Both of these women captured huge audiences for their television shows through the sharing of their most personal stories (although giving away cars to audience members also helped!).

In his book *New Vision, New Directions: Implementing the Catechism of the Catholic Church* (Allen, TX: Thomas More, 1994), Robert Hater identifies the desire for intimacy and quest for community as two of the most driving needs within our culture today. Such concerns are compelling parishes to look at how they are bringing people together in ways that foster interaction, facilitate relationships, and cultivate a sense of belonging.

Enculturation is a two-way street. As defined in the *General Directory for Catechesis* (GDC), it means that the Church is not only mindful of the cultural milieu of its people but is also influenced by it. Pop culture is, of course, only one aspect of this vast milieu. Other deeper cultural influences, such as family or ethnicity, profoundly mark the people with whom we minister. It makes for the rich tapestry of color within the fabric of the Church.

What they care about

I once held a position as ministry coordinator in a large suburban parish populated with a number of young families. One of my responsibilities was planning and implementing the baptismal preparation program. Since we averaged one infant baptism per week, this was no small task. Most of the parents came to inquire about baptism after the child was born. As is the case in many communities, they were also returning to active involvement in the Church after a prolonged lapse that started in late adolescence. The pastor and I both agreed that the baptism of their children was a golden moment, a window of opportunity in which to welcome the entire family into the faith community.

As I planned the sessions, I tried to incorporate group dynamics that would help parents get to know one another. I came up with a number of questions to initiate dialogue. These ranged from "What do you want for your child?" to surfacing their questions about the baptismal rite. No matter what I proposed, however, I noticed that the discussion in all groups gravitated to one particular topic: the labor and delivery process. After a few meetings it began to dawn on me how the parents were naturally drawn toward the topic that was most meaningful to them and was also very pertinent to baptism: the mystery and miracle of life. I eventually wised up and started to pose this as an opening discussion—i.e., tell a story about the anticipated or actual birth or adoption of your child.

This is a kind of "stand-in-the-back" approach to ministry. In retail work, sales managers often "shop" in their own stores in order to see them from the viewpoint of a customer. This can be a very beneficial way for a minister to look at his or her parish. If we made it a point, perhaps over a period of two months, to attend each of the weekend liturgies and one parish meeting as an observer, what would we see? What would excite us? What would frustrate us? How would we feel included or excluded? What would we notice about the way people enter, are greeted, participate, and depart? Such an exercise provides a bit of the context that was mentioned in Chapter 3 as the starting point for good planning.

Another of Hater's critical needs is that of a yearning for certitude and roots. This may be one of the underlying issues beneath Kevin's scenario. Catholicism is a religion that places great stock in its symbols and rituals. We cannot afford to be careless with them and, when we are, the reaction can be swift and fierce. Whether it's eliminating an Advent wreath, moving a statue, or painting the church, the furor it sets off can leave us, like Kevin, surprised and perplexed. Why does it matter so much?

In the case of the mountain parish, the pastor recognized the need to honor the feelings and memories of his parishioners. The town was going through a financial depression after a major industry shut its doors and left many people unemployed. Families were moving away or being torn apart by increases in divorces and addictions. Suicides among youth were on the rise. The church paintings represented much more than warm, fuzzy memories of a bygone pastor. They spoke of better days and represented the tenacity and enduring strength of the community to weather the good times and the bad.

In Kevin's case, the outrage over the Advent wreath could be attributed to a perception that no one was consulted about the decision. It may spring from a "we've always done it this way" mindset. As the baptismal parents taught me, however, there is often much more to the story. Perhaps, at some level, the lighting of the wreath provides a tangible connection between parish and family. After all, it started out as a home-based symbol. The wreath represents an essential meaning of Advent—the coming of Christ into a world that desperately needs light. It makes a religious ritual accessible and understandable for all ages.

None of this means that pastoral ministers shouldn't be holding to the integrity of liturgical rites, symbols, and traditions. Nor does it preclude the introduction of new ways of thinking, acting, praying, and worshiping. What I have learned along my ministerial way is that people know much more than we give them credit for and that we can learn a lot about effective ministry by taking our lead from them.

We must also be aware that the demise of the Fr. O'Malley days means that the parish is no longer the central locale for spiritual and religious resources. A Gallup study conducted in the mid-1990s, and reported in Phyllis Tickle's *Re-Discovering the Sacred* (New York: Crossroad, 1995), projected that the largest sales increase in nonfiction books in the first part of the twenty-first century would be in the area of religion and spirituality. The study predicted an 82% growth rate from 1987 to 2010. This project did not take into account the massive impact and potential of the Internet. For instance, as of August 3, 2011, Amazon.com revealed the following search results:

- ▶ 141,201 books were found under the heading "spirituality"
- ▶ 765,517 books were found under the heading "religion"
- ▶ 281,690 books were found under the heading "Christianity"

Not only can I buy these books over the web or download them to my computer, tablet or even my phone, I can join an online group to discuss them. This raises all sorts of exciting possibilities for parishes, especially in the area of adult faith formation. It also means "logging on" and listening in greater depth to what parishioners are being drawn to. Tickle mentions four major trends in contemporary spiritual/religious publishing: near-death experiences, books of ancient wisdom, self-help, and faith fiction. Some of these trends are right up our ministerial alley. The resurgence of interest in wisdom literature means that resources on Scripture and the writings of saints and mystics are in great demand. A weekly glance at a local or national best-seller list always shows at least two or three titles that could be identified as self-help. These are often grounded in some aspect of meditation, prayer, and interior reflection.

The longings that fuel these popular trends are as old as human history. We continue to struggle with our losses and our loneliness, with our questions and our quests, and with our desire to connect with one another.

When I served as a parish life coordinator, I used to offer reflections at Mass on occasion. These talks were well received, probably because I always included something that related to ordinary life. Since leaving that position over ten years ago, I am still approached on occasion by parishioners in the grocery store or at the gym. They ask how I am and what I am doing. Inevitably, someone will tell me they miss my stories. Not my insights, my ideas, or my leadership. They miss the stories.

Over the years, fine-tuning my approach to ministry, as well as to my writing, speaking, and spiritual direction, has involved a growing awareness of the day-to-day lives of the people I serve—who they are, what they do, and what they care about. It's one of the most vital things I know about parish ministry.

CHAPTER 5

Collaboration

"Why can't I just do it myself?"

Scenario

Rita receives a rather unpleasant surprise when she goes to the parish office to pick up her mail. Scanning the bulletin for the upcoming week, she notices an announcement for Back to School night. It's scheduled at the same time and in the same place as her weekly choir rehearsal. With the need to practice new Advent music, this is going to pose a major problem. She gets little sympathy from the parish secretary who manages both facility usage and the parish calendar. "It wasn't in the book," she shrugs.

Rita seethes as she leaves the office. As a part-time employee it isn't always possible for her to get to staff meetings. She suspects the secretary of being devious in her decision to give the space to the school. "She did it on purpose," Rita fumes to herself. "After all, everyone knows choir rehearsal is on Tuesday."

Your thoughts

? What went wrong?

? What assumptions did Rita make about other members of the staff?

? How could this situation be avoided?

? Do you think the secretary was being devious? What would give her cause to be?

What makes collaboration so hard?

The summer comes to an end, and everyone on the parish staff wants to make a fresh start. There is talk about being a "team." There is hope that new members on staff or committees will make the group more cohesive. As the weeks pass, communication begins to flag under the pressure of day-to-day responsibilities and multiplying demands. Clashes of will and work style begin to emerge, and the great vision of collaboration fades. By spring old patterns have taken hold. The primary agenda at staff meetings is now to share individual calendar dates. The excitement and enthusiasm of working together is gone.

Collaboration is of tremendous interest to pastoral ministers. Most of us really want to work together and are desperately disappointed when it doesn't happen. Maybe this desire arises from a view of the Church as an institution in which, above all, we should be able to orchestrate our efforts around a common purpose. The emergence of new ministries after Vatican II led to great expectations about how clergy and laity would work together. These have been harder to reach than we thought.

I have devoted a good deal of time to the topic of collaboration over the past several years. This entailed helping others learn what it means and how it can be accomplished. I have also experienced volunteer and staff situations at both the parish and diocesan levels in which attempts at collaborating have either succeeded dramatically or failed dismally. My experience has taught me four things:

▶ Most of us aren't really sure what collaboration is.

▶ Most of us aren't really prepared for what collaboration unleashes.

▶ Most of us aren't really aware of what makes collaboration fail.

▶ All of us are curious about what makes collaboration work.

There is a classic scene in Woody Allen's 1969 movie *Take the Money and Run.* Six convicts who are chained together at the ankle escape a chain gang by simply running over a hill. They make it to a farmhouse and try to convince the owner that they are cousins even though each one is a different size, shape, and color. When one asks to use the bathroom, the rest shuffle along behind him, trying to look as nonchalant as possible.

This might be the mental view many of us have about collaboration—a chained-at-the-ankle experience. Even if we like each other a lot, the idea of being together all the time is not very appealing. We need to be realistic about what collaboration is and how it can be configured.

Loughlan Sofield, ST, and Carroll Juliano, SHCJ, define collaboration as "the identification, release, and union of all the gifts of ministry for the sake of mission" (*Collaboration: Uniting Our Gifts in Ministry*, Notre Dame, IN: Ave Maria Press, 2000). It is indeed a gift to find a collaborative partner—someone with whom to share ideas and visions, plans and implementation. Most pastoral "teams" don't automatically click, however. They need to learn how to work together. They also need to determine how much collaborating they really want to do.

Although it was published in 1986, Dr. Bernard Swain's book *Liberating Leadership* (San Francisco: Harper & Row, 1986) serves as a helpful look at collaboration. In it, Swain describes four basic styles of pastoral leadership that emerged in the Church before and after Vatican II:

1. Sovereign. Predominant in the Church prior to Vatican II, this style typified the way parishes were structured, with the pastor as the supreme authority. It is a simple and efficient model. Not much time is wasted in meetings! It is also an effective way to handle crisis situations. As one school principal told me, "When the fire alarm goes off, I am the sovereign leader." On the other hand, this style inhibits growth and creativity and tends to keep others—coworkers and parishioners—in a passive role.

2. Parallel. As the word implies, this style fits for systems in which each person operates independently of one another. It emerged in the mid-1960s as new ministries took hold in parishes. The style is also simple and provides more room than the sovereign model for pastoral ministers to excel in their area of expertise. Complications arise when separate planning and implementation cross one another. Rita's scenario is a perfect example.

3. Semi-mutual. With this style, planning is done in concert with others while implementation takes place separately. As such, it is a blend of the parallel and mutual models and derives benefits from each: the creativity of joint planning and the autonomy that allows people to carry out their work on their own.

4. Mutual. Retreat teams provide a good example of this model. They plan and implement their work together. This can be an extremely rewarding experience—and also tremendously time-consuming. The more mutual the leadership style, the less efficient it is. Meetings compound and fewer things can be accomplished. But it can also be a more effective way to work when coordination and cohesiveness are values of the group.

Swain presents each of the four styles in pure form but notes that we tend to combine them into a "recipe" as circumstances warrant. Each of us has a preference for one style over the others. We are satisfied or dissatisfied to the degree that we are able to work out of our preferred style. Uncovering these preferences can be most enlightening.

I have drawn upon Swain's book for years when facilitating leadership workshops, and I usually find that a group's *expectation* of collaborative ministry is based on the mutual style of leadership. Shared planning and implementation are named as the way in which collaboration "should" operate. Their *preference* for ministry, however, is generally semi-mutual. If their situation is especially harried, they seem to veer towards the parallel style, noting how much easier it is to work on your own.

In Chapter 1, we looked at the frustration that results when there is a lack of congruence between how we prefer to work and the actual demands of our job. It is the same for working with others. Swain's four styles of leadership shed some light on why collaboration succeeds or fails. By naming different ways of working together, it helps us identify the recipe that works best for each of us. It also uncovers perceptions about collaboration itself.

What have we gotten ourselves into?

Several years ago I facilitated a team day for a parish staff. At one point I asked each person to list his or her hopes for collaborative ministry. Everyone expressed an interest in working together more intentionally as well as in shared decision making. The pastor listened to the dialogue intently. Finally, he expressed his own dilemma. "I hear what you're saying, but when it comes to final decisions about the parish, the buck stops here. I'm the one who has to answer to the bishop." He was caught between the expectations of his staff and an institutional system that holds the pastor directly responsible for the management of a parish. There were times, he explained, when he had to be a sovereign leader.

What does this mean for teamwork? A great deal depends upon the person in charge. I know many pastors and parish directors who are eager to foster a collaborative spirit among staff and other parish leaders. It just isn't always possible. In the scenario described above, the pastor's willingness to articulate his predicament was invaluable to his staff. It moved the entire group toward greater realism about their expectations. It also helped the pastor name specific ways in which collaboration and shared decision making could work without compromising his authority.

There are major tensions that sit like land mines in parishes over this issue. Some people want total collegiality in making decisions and laying out plans. Others are just as happy to "let Father do it." When these expectations collide, it makes for spectacular fireworks. There are serious ramifications to being collaborative. We may be about the same task or goal as we were thirty years ago, but the way we are going to achieve it has shifted.

The way we relate to one another is different as well. The movement from a sovereign to a mutual style of leadership changes the "direction" of accountability. Simply put, it goes from being more vertical (employee to supervisor) to horizontal (team members to one another). This is a dramatic change in the way many people are used to seeing the Church work. It explains the conflicts that arise when a group is promised a "team" approach to something and the pastor then "pulls rank" and makes a sovereign decision. He may be perfectly free to do so, but the group had entirely different expectations. When this happens regularly, cynicism and disillusionment result.

This also works in reverse. A youth ministry coordinator once told me that she resented top-down approaches to ministry except when it was "convenient." In other words, when tough or unpleasant circumstances arose, it was easier for her to duck behind the authority of the pastor and to let him be the bad guy. As Fr. William Bausch put it in his *The Total Parish Manual* (Mystic, CT: Twenty-Third Publications, 1994): "As long as Father is superior, we don't have to be responsible...In a word, we unconsciously foster co-dependency."

We meant well—what happened?

If you've been in ministry longer than a month, you have probably had a "Rita" experience. Someone usurps a date or a decision. You have a run-in with a staff or committee member. You get involved in a "turf war" with another ministry or organization. Any one of these things can lead us to conclude that our efforts at cooperation have failed. It's more likely that a combination of factors has inhibited the spirit of collaboration. These could include the following:

1. Change. I'm a big fan of Fred Astaire and Ginger Rogers. Combined with a Cole Porter score, there is no better formula for a great musical. Fred and Ginger fit together. Their dance steps were in perfect sync even though Ginger, as she so aptly described, had to do it all "backwards and in high heels." Both had other dancing partners in their careers, but nothing seemed to match the style and grace that emerged when they were together.

If we are lucky—very lucky—we will get a chance to dance in ministry like Astaire and Rogers. We will be part of a magical configuration where our preferred work styles complement each other, our visions of Church converge, and our ability to serve as a catalyst for one another's creativity will soar. Then one person leaves and a new one enters. Things just don't work so well anymore.

When the participants change, so, too, does the dance. As a matter of fact, the subject of breaking in a new partner was the plot line for several of Fred Astaire's movies. It was never an easy process, and he often discovered great talent lying dormant in the most unlikely candidates.

When new people come onto a staff, council, or committee, they bring their own set of expectations and ideas. The dance shifts and we must be willing to listen to our new partners, allowing time for adjustment to different rhythms. Conversely, new team members need to respect the past work and experience of the group into which they are moving. Change is an ongoing part of parish life.

The better able we are to adapt, the greater our chances of moving through it gracefully.

2. Assumptions. "Everyone knows choir rehearsal is on Tuesdays." Rita's assumption set off a chain of reactions that eventually came round to smack her in the face. The secretary may very well have given the space to the school "on purpose," as Rita suspected. On the other hand, she might have been on overload herself and, without the choir rehearsal written on the calendar, would not have considered it. If Rita changed her plans, how was the secretary to know?

Aside from these day-to-day assumptions, there are larger ones about collaboration. Prior to facilitating another parish workshop, I was told by the DRE that everyone on staff was enthusiastically committed to the concept of collaborative ministry. I presented Swain's four styles and then asked each staff member to identify his or her preference. The pastor and worship director were the only ones who named the semi-mutual and mutual models. Everyone else, including the DRE, named the parallel style. We may assume "everyone" wants to collaborate, but what that means varies from one person to the next.

3. People. Some of us just don't know how to collaborate. We may have the best intentions in the world, but if our primary experience has been working in a sovereign or parallel situation, we may not know what collaboration entails.

There are also people who aren't easy to work with. These are the ones who put up roadblocks through their attitudes and behaviors. An example of this is the "lone ranger" who is situated in the midst of a cheerleading squad. You know the type—the ones who insist upon doing their own moves and using their own kind of music. They plan by themselves, are reticent (and sometimes duplicitous) about sharing information, and schedule events on top of someone else's. It is a frustrating problem that can generate two different reactions. The first is trying to ignore the lone ranger while simultaneously building up a boatload of internal resentment. The other is going overboard by trying to include her in our plans. The hope is that she will be converted and reciprocity will be the end result. It usually doesn't happen.

It is better to let go, to move on, and to find others with whom we can collaborate. When the lone ranger creates problems for larger plans, it is important to confront the situation rather than suffer in silence. For example, Rita left the office instead of asking the secretary about the scheduling conflict. She's not likely to know the intent unless she asks.

The pessimist is another example of a problem person who abounds in church work. They cast a pall over everything with their "it will never work" attitude. The extreme pessimist needs to be challenged about his continual role in ministry. If things are so hopeless, why does he stay? It is important to monitor our own attitudes on a regular basis in order to check for signs of pessimism and cynicism.

4. Conflict. Max De Pree notes in his book *Leadership Is an Art* (New York: Dell Publishing, 1989): "Three of the key elements in the art of working together are how to deal with change, how to deal with conflict, and how to realize our potential." Chapter 9 deals with conflict in greater depth. It is essential to note here, however, that the more effectively we deal with conflict in a healthy manner, the better the chances for collaborative ministry.

5. Time. The demands on our time sometimes make collaborative ministry an unachievable goal. Many of us have so much to do that the thought of collaboration seems like a luxury. The irony here, of course, is that we should actually save time by pairing our efforts and sharing the load. In many cases, a team is not willing to give the kind of front-end time for visioning and planning that makes this work. Without it we will never know what gifts, interests, and availability we each have to share with one another.

Seven ways to make collaboration work

1. Clarity. Here is a quick checklist that can remind us of what we need in order to work together:

▶ Does everyone understand what needs to be done? Are goals, objectives, and strategies clear?

▶ Have we been educated to the task, and do we know how to fulfill the expectations of the team and the parish at large?

▶ Is sufficient information available to help us accomplish our task?

▶ Are there timelines and milestones so that each of us knows if we are on track?

▶ Are times set aside to evaluate our work together?

▶ Is there ready praise for tasks accomplished, and re-grouping and re-directing of energies when things are not on track?

▶ Does everyone feel trusted and supported?

"You better think about what you're trying to do to me."

— ARETHA FRANKLIN

---

2. Consideration. In order to be collaborative, it is important to continually think "system," to consider the parish as a whole. Breaking this down even further, here are particular people who must be considered:

Parishioners. In Chapter 4 we looked at ways to be more attentive to the needs and interests of the people in the parish. Collaboration always considers how plans will affect the community at large. Is my work facilitating the active participation of the parishioners in a life of faith and witness? Am I working in such a way that my plans will not create conflict and confusion with other parish ministries?

Coworkers. How will my plans affect those with whom I work? Will my plans complement their work or compete with it? What gifts and abilities are present among staff, committee members, and volunteers that will enhance my ministry?

Consideration of coworkers includes the assistance we can extend to them. How will collaboration lighten everyone's workload and benefit the parish at large? How can I promote other ministries? What do I know about the jobs of others? Did Rita, for example, stop to consider what the secretary goes through when everyone is vying for limited space on an already overcrowded calendar? Showing others that we respect and honor what they do strengthens relationships and promotes congeniality.

Volunteers. Who is there to help and in what capacity? Will my own plans draw volunteers away from another ministry and thus create conflicts? Am I working with others to make sure that no one person is being asked to do too much?

3. Calendar. Good collaboration involves attentiveness to time. Consider both the parish and the home calendar. Do my programs back up against something else in the parish? Am I competing for people's time, forcing them to choose between programs in the parish, or between church and family? Ideally the parish calendar is created through a process of joint planning with staff and other parish leadership. If this is not possible, we can initiate the process ourselves by consulting with others who are involved in ministerial planning.

"Power must be shared for an organization or a relationship to work."   — MAX DE PREE

---

4. Consultation. Like it or not, collaboration includes meetings. We have to continually consult with a large number of people in order to be effective. Sometimes this multiplies our work; other times it may condense it. A consultant network—people we can rely on for ideas, input, and feedback—involves people from various backgrounds and with different interests and levels of parish involvement. It helps to talk to colleagues—ministers from other parishes—who might lend a practical yet "outside" eye to what we are doing.

"It's hard to rally around ambiguity."
—GEORGE WHALEN, FRIEND AND MENTOR

---

5. Communication. This is the area where collaboration often breaks down. We ask others what they think and then do not consider what they need to know afterwards. Poor communication is one of the most frequent sources of misunderstanding and conflict in parish life. It is important to share regular updates on our work and programs with coworkers—via meetings, memos, and promotional materials, interoffice email or voice mail systems.

Keeping the "forgotten players" like the secretary in the loop enables them to answer phone calls and keep bulletin and website information up to date. Talking to those in charge of maintaining the parish facilities assures that our needs for set-up and take-down, equipment, heating or cooling are taken care of. Letting them know well in advance means we don't consider them less important in the collaborative circle.

It is often these levels of communication that are most neglected. Failing to put an event on the calendar, as in Rita's case, leads to bad feelings and scrambled efforts to rectify mistakes. We must not forget to let all of these people know of changes in our plans as well. And, of course, a thank-you note or comment goes a long way in recognizing the work that has gone on behind the scenes to make our efforts successful.

"The real mystery of music-making requires real friendship among those who work together."

— CARLO MARIA GIULINI, FORMER CONDUCTOR
LOS ANGELES PHILHARMONIC

6. Cohesiveness. As Ronald Rolheiser points out in his book *The Holy Longing* (New York: Doubleday, 1999), "The group of disciples that first gathered around Jesus were not individuals who were mutually compatible at all." They came from different backgrounds and had different temperaments and different visions of what Jesus was all about. Petty squabbles have been part of the Church since its inception. Coming together is a time-consuming process that involves building trust, support, and mutual respect.

Ann McGee-Cooper, in writing about time management, notes the need for a "balancing partner." Otherwise, she says, we end up sabotaging ourselves by focusing exclusively on our own talents. Recognizing and affirming the strengths in the other that complement mine or offset my weaknesses is part of the process. So, too, is developing an understanding of the way others work. Something as simple as studying others' desks or workspaces can give us a glimpse into how they work and what they value.

"The group will not prosper if the leader grabs the lion's share of the credit for the good work that has been done."

— LAO-TZU

7. Celebration. Lao-tzu's bit of wisdom is certainly true in the Church. The trouble in pastoral ministry is that no one is taking much credit because we don't stop long enough to celebrate our successes. Good teams know how to genuinely laugh and to affirm one another. They take time to revel in the good work they've done and to recognize their mistakes as opportunities for growth. They understand celebration as a necessity for working together, not a luxury.

"I believe it's a sin to make things last forever.
Everything that exists in time runs out of time someday.
Got to let go of the things that keep you tethered.
Take your place with grace and then be on your way."
— BRUCE COCKBURN, "MIGHTY TRUCKS AT MIDNIGHT"
(ON HIS CD *NOTHING BUT A BURNING LIGHT*)

When to let go

One of my most rewarding experiences of collaboration occurred while I was working as the director of religious education for the Diocese of Colorado Springs. The bishop and his staff developed a long-range plan that included leadership development in the areas of religious education, youth, family, and social ministries. It was a small diocese and each of these areas had only one person dedicated to it. Therefore we implemented a team approach. Dubbing ourselves the Rainbow Connection, we set out with great enthusiasm to accomplish the diocesan goal.

We worked well together and spent a good deal of time discerning our roles and vision, brainstorming ideas, and figuring out the logistics of a collaborative model. How often should we meet? Who should chair meetings? Who has the final say in what the group does or doesn't decide to do? We weren't always in sync, but we had an inherent respect for one another and a true enjoyment in being together. We began socializing with our families outside of work, and the bonds grew stronger.

After a couple of years, two of the team members left to pursue other areas of ministry. It was daunting for their replacements to enter a group as close as ours. Things did not go smoothly. Styles clashed, conflicts arose, and meetings dragged on with excruciating effort at figuring out ways to work together. After one long and difficult planning session, we decided to disband.

I went home that evening feeling both drained and disappointed, and listened repeatedly to Cockburn's song about change. Nothing does last forever, and the best thing we can do is "take our place with grace" and then move on. I had to let go of something I cared about, and it took time to grieve its loss. New configurations rose out of the ashes of the Rainbow Connection as different people came together in a continued, albeit altered, form of collaboration. I formed a particularly close working relationship with the director of youth ministry. For the next few years we created some dynamic leadership programs together and had a lot of fun in the process.

In *The Holy Longing*, Rolheiser writes, "Christian spirituality is as much about dealing with each other as it is about dealing with God." So is collaboration. We are, quite simply, not meant to go it alone.

CHAPTER 6

Coworkers

"I'd like an office in the bell tower, please"

Scenario

Steven sinks into his favorite chair and pops open a beer. His head is throbbing, but he feels too exhausted to climb the stairs for an aspirin. Tonight's pastoral council meeting was a disaster, and he wonders about his continued commitment as chairperson. He runs over it in his mind, and it seems even more chaotic in hindsight.

One particularly outspoken member sidelined the agenda by bringing up—again—the need to repave the parking lot. Another was just as vehement about using the money to fund a camping trip for the youth group. Two of the quieter members sided with whoever was the loudest. One woman arrived thirty minutes late, and the group had to backtrack to catch her up on the discussion at hand. The "parking lot advocate" seemed determined to run the meeting, and Steven felt inadequate in his ability to restore order. The pastor, meanwhile, said nothing all evening except leading the group in a closing prayer. It was a great relief for Steven when he was able to say "Amen" and rush out to his car.

The council started the year with such promise. There was camaraderie, and everyone seemed committed to working for the best interests of the parish. Now it seems to degenerate into power plays and personal agendas.

"What is going on?" Steven asks himself as he drains the last of his beer. "Aren't we all supposed to work together?"

Your thoughts

? Have you ever been to a meeting like this?

? How do you handle people who sideline the group with their own agenda?

? What does it take to work together?

? What type of people do you have the most trouble working with?

Taking the plunge

"I am so tired of going to workshops on collaboration," a parish minister once said to me. "When are we just going to start doing it?"

Several months later, I was involved in helping this same woman's parish staff resolve some deep issues of conflict. On my first visit, I noticed that she had chosen an office in the old school building, far removed from the rest of the staff. It was a striking illustration of her actual attitude toward working with others. There is a vast difference between wanting to collaborate and actually doing it. As Loughlan Sofield and Carroll Juliano point out, "The desire must be accompanied by a willingness to invest time, energy, and one's self if collaboration is to succeed." Taking an office in the bell tower is not a good first step.

The frustration this woman expressed is common among pastoral workers. The way she phrased it, however, belies an inherent attitudinal problem. It sees collaborative ministry as something that "happens" as opposed to something in which we actively participate. Working together, as Steven experienced, is a hard and uneven process. It takes commitment to making the group cohesive and a willingness to work with difficult people. It also means being honest with ourselves in order to see where our own skills as a coworker need some adjustment.

Reaching a point of corporate harmony is a step-by-step process. Recognizing these steps can help promote a more realistic understanding of how collaboration works.

The journey toward harmony

1. Gathering
2. Gelling
3. Colliding
4. Teaming

Group development

There are various ways to describe how to develop a harmonious group. This is how I see it taking place.

1. Gathering. Steven's memories of the early stages of camaraderie among the pastoral council members are not unlike what many of us experience when a committee or staff first comes together. Unless we have been coerced into participation, we tend to enter groups with the best of intentions—open to knowing one another and anxious to learn about our task. Charles Keating says, "If there are hidden agendas, they generally remain hidden and do not affect behavior." This is a polite stage that may involve testing the waters in order to see what the group is like and how one does or does not fit in. It is an important first step in working together because time is needed to become acquainted.

2. Gelling. This stage often follows the first one rather quickly. Once we have become comfortable with one another, we start to explore our purpose. We move beyond polite behavior and tell each other our own particular interests as well as our concerns. With the help of effective leadership, the group is able to clarify its purpose and lay aside issues that are peripheral or inappropriate.

3. Colliding. Steven's suspicion that one of the council members was trying to wrest control of the meeting was probably dead-on. Power plays are an attempt, often by well-meaning people, to "set the group right." In parishes where parishioners hold high-powered jobs in the business world, this tendency to take charge can be even more prevalent. Personality clashes, differences in work styles, and varying visions of church are all likely to appear at this stage. It takes strong leadership to help the group move to the next stage. Otherwise, development is stymied or destroyed altogether.

4. Teaming. Once a group reaches this step, they learn to lay aside personal agendas in order to work together. They come to a point of valuing cooperation, sharing, and active listening. Group motivation is high, and responsibilities are shared in an equal way. Collisions may still occur, but the group has learned how to work with them. The leader takes a backseat role at this point, monitoring any signs of regression and providing for the logistical needs of the group.

Many parish leaders assume that "teaming" is the first step in collaboration. They start the year with "team-building" exercises and activities—long before the group has really named these as values. In fact, moving to the fourth step of group development requires long-term investment in building relationships.

Building good working relationships

Loughlan Sofield is widely respected for his extensive work in the area of pastoral ministry and leadership. He notes that, when asked to name the biggest obstacles to collaborative ministry, most of his workshop participants place "other people" at the top of the list.

This response deflects the problem by foisting it onto others. It's moving into the bell tower in the hopes that when you come down, everyone else will suddenly have become magically enlightened and collaboration, at last, will work.

Moving to the fourth step of group development requires the building of relationships. Here are some ways to do this.

1. Embrace our gifts. In all my years of working with pastoral ministry, I cannot recall ever being part of a gift discernment process. I've participated in lots of workshops on personality typology, work styles, and strength/weakness indicators. A gift is something different. In the first letter to the Corinthians there is a beautiful explanation of the different gifts that are given to the community, all emanating from the same Spirit (1 Corinthians 12).

> *Any group that wishes to minister collaboratively must seriously engage in an ongoing process of gift discernment and acquire mechanisms to fully employ those gifts in a common mission.* — LOUGHLAN SOFIELD AND CARROLL JULIANO

Whatever our situation, it is vital to embrace the gifts we have and to use them as much as possible in our work. This is no place for false modesty or for competition. Our mission as Christian ministers impels us to use our gifts for the good of the community

2. Help others grow. Acknowledging, affirming, and utilizing the gifts of others is one way to help them grow. I once had a coworker who told me she kept a "wonderful things" file. When someone sent her a note or paid her a compliment, she stuck it in the file. She pulled it out and went through it on days when she felt discouraged and inadequate. "My confidence is always restored through this process," she told me, "and I am motivated anew by the faith others have in me."

"Many people look at themselves, and they look at others, and they think that the way to get bigger themselves is to get others down to size, make others smaller. So they start to nibble."

— KALEEL JAMISON,
THE NIBBLE THEORY AND THE KERNEL OF POWER

She was also given to sending notes to others in order to affirm their work. Having experienced the generosity of her coworkers, she was thus enabled to be more lavish in her affirmation of others.

This is the opposite of nibbling. It is a way to build others up through heartfelt words of encouragement.

3. Let go of grudges. I once worked in a diocese where, before my time, the bishop had to close the only Catholic high school due to financial problems. The decision was received with great difficulty by many of the parents, and resentments festered for years afterward. Occasionally I ran into someone on a committee or at a workshop who still seethed over the issue even though a creative alternative eventually emerged from the closure. The inability to let this matter go made these people perpetually angry and poisoned the atmosphere around them.

There is no question that conflict is a part of parish life and work. One might even say it is a necessary component because it points to a community that is dynamic rather than stagnant. The maintenance of grudges, however, only serves to drag us down and stifles our abilities to work with others. Dr. Frederic Luskin, founder of the Stanford Forgiveness Project, recommends a way to deal with grudges. Spend a half hour each day in solitude, focusing on those things—or people—that irritate, annoy, or upset us. Luskin predicts that, after a few sessions, we will grow so weary of those negative thoughts that we will be ready to move on and let it all go. There is enough weight on our shoulders without the added burden of past resentments.

4. Stay focused on serving human needs. "If you've entered ministry to get your own needs met, you will never survive." When I heard those words from a retreat director a few years ago, I was struggling to keep my head above water as a parish life coordinator. It was Holy Week and the strain of being in charge was weighing heavily upon me. The closer we moved toward the Triduum, however, the better I began to feel. The efforts of staff, committees, liturgical ministers, RCIA team, and musicians were coming together, and the joint effort set the stage for a beautiful liturgical celebration. When a tearful woman approached me after the Good Friday service to tell me it was the most spiritual experience of her life, I tasted once again the fruit of collaborative ministry.

Maintaining a broader vision and focusing on the service of others is what ministry is all about. Some of us may have been propelled into ministry in the first place by our own needs and concerns. What ultimately keeps us in it—at least in a healthy way—is the opportunity to be of service to others.

5. Keep a sense of humor. In Chapter 3 I related a story about inheriting the coordination of a rather fractious parish event. As the tensions between the different groups grew, I was fielding phone calls each day over one concern or another. The last straw came when one woman called to tell me the conflict was a sign that God didn't want us to play bingo.

In desperation I called the pastor. His steadiness and humor always provided a sense of balance, and I knew he would offer wise counsel. After describing the latest phone call, I asked if he thought God really didn't want us to play bingo. "Frankly," he laughed, "I don't think God gives a damn."

It wasn't quite the answer I was expecting, but it did turn out to be "wise counsel." Years later, my husband put it another way: "Develop thick skin and ignore half of what is going on." Doing so with a smile is even better.

6. Follow good example. The aforementioned pastor continued to inspire me as I moved into more intense levels of ministry.

It was not just his sense of humor, but the genuine love he had for his vocation and for the people he served. I can count many other people who provided examples of what it means to be a compassionate and caring minister. Our Church has long honored saints as role models and witnesses to the faith. It is the people close at hand, those everyday saints, who teach us on a daily basis what it means to be an effective coworker.

"It is inconceivable to expect collaborative ministry to occur when the individuals working together do not share faith."

— LOUGHLAN SOFIELD AND CARROLL JULIANO

7. Share faith. Faith-sharing entails more than an obligatory prayer at the start and end of a meeting. During the years I worked for the Diocese of Colorado Springs, time was set aside every Thursday morning for prayer. Open to all, but not required, it gave everyone from the bishop to the bookkeeper a chance to come together in faith. When we went through personal tragedies or diocesan crises, these prayer gatherings became our greatest source of strength and unity. I credit those weekly gatherings with the spirit of camaraderie that pervaded the entire office.

8. Be sensitive to loss. Failure to deal honestly and openly with loss can have a devastating effect on the entire system. We can be awfully careless with this in our parishes. Pastors are reassigned without enough notice to allow parishioners to say good-bye. A staff member leaves, and there is no acknowledgment of her past work and commitment to the community. A coworker experiences a death in his family, and no one says anything for fear of "upsetting" him.

These losses are like the elephant in the living room. They have a deep impact on relationships and our capacity to work with others, especially when we fail to acknowledge them. Being a good coworker means sharing our own losses and encouraging others to do the same.

How to work with difficult people

So...we've done all sorts of soul-searching about our styles and our attitudes. We discerned our gifts and tried to affirm the gifts of others. We listen and we care, and we maintain a sense of humor and seek the counsel of others. Why is it still so hard to work with some people?

M. Scott Peck started his classic book, *The Road Less Traveled*, with a simple acknowledgement: "Life is difficult." What makes it so is the need to interact with others. Steven finds this out while chairing the parish council. A pastoral minister sought to alleviate her situation by seeking an office in a remote part of the building. Some people are very difficult to work with, and the efforts we expend in trying to get along with them can be enormous.

All sorts of books have been written on the various types of difficult people. Here is a list of my own and what I wish I had known when I first started parish ministry. It might have spared me a lot of time, stress, and grief.

1. The controller. Many of us have experienced something like Steven's encounter with the "parking lot advocate." We leave a meeting and spend the rest of the night stewing over the behavior of someone who tried to take over or who rubbed us the wrong way with an attitude of arrogance and self-righteousness. This may involve hierarchical roles—the clergymen or women religious who see themselves as superior to others who are "just" laypersons, for example. It may be the assumption that one's education or experience entitles someone to more of an opinion than others. Sofield and Juliano state it well: "Arrogant people are not attracted to collaboration because they don't see the need for the gifts of anyone else."

The paradox of the controller is that she may actually struggle with low self-esteem or a lack of self-confidence, thus necessitating the façade of appearing to be superior to those she leads. Position, however, does not necessarily mean competence. The more inadequate a person feels, the more he may try to operate out of a sense of absolute control.

Controllers often feel the need to be in the know. Thus, including them in the circulation of information can improve working relationships. They also need feedback, especially on what they do well.

2. The saboteur. The flip side to the controller is the person who is agreeable to almost anything we propose. We leave a meeting thinking that all is in order and then find out a few days later that our affable coworker has gone ahead with his own plans and disregarded the work we completed together.

Saboteurs are classic passive-aggressive personalities. They often fear conflict and will agree to anything in order to keep the peace. One way to deal with these people is to challenge them. This need not be confrontational or rude. It is more of an honest questioning that states in simple terms our own sense of confusion about what has transpired. As such, challenging the saboteur also means being willing to listen to his side of things. This is time-consuming and requires a commitment to improving the working relationship.

3. The moocher. Moochers are more than content to let you do all the work. They come along for the ride and enjoy reaping the rewards of a job well done (by you).

Several years ago, I was exasperated by an experience with a moocher. After a long and arduous tirade, a friend and mentor caught me up short with her response. "You've got to remember that most people are dull," she told me. There is much truth to this. It doesn't mean that people are stupid. Rather, they are dulled by the workloads they manage and the responsibilities they shoulder. Some are simply not good at generating ideas. They are the pruners described in Chapter 1.

An awareness of the many and varied gifts we each bring to ministry can help transform our view of the moocher to one of maintainer. They often just want to know when and how to contribute. Max De Pree calls them "catchers" and points out that every good pitcher is in need of one.

4. The vexer. Like fingernails scraping across a blackboard, vexers make the hair on the back of the neck stand on end. Their vocal expressions and behaviors are just plain annoying. Whether they affect the atmosphere of an entire room or just my own space, they are hard to be around and excruciating to work with. On top of that, we feel guilty for being so negative and then try to talk ourselves into feeling better about them. After all, can they help being who they are?

An effective way to deal with these attitudes is through compassion. It may entail hearing a simple story about their lives or touching upon a point of mutual understanding that helps us view them in a different light.

5. The prima donna. We are all likely to come face-to-face with this type of person at one time or another. They are the ones who want the office with the view or coffee served at a certain temperature. They don't "do" certain things like move chairs or clean up the lunchroom. Their own needs are always more pressing than those of anyone else.

The prima donna needs a healthy dose of humility, and many of us are more than happy to dish it up. In her book *Emotional Alchemy: How the Mind Can Heal the Heart* (New York: Harmony Books, 2001), Tara Bennett-Goleman describes these people as seeing themselves entitled to special treatment. This may stem from being spoiled as children and treated as a little prince or princess. Their behavior can also stem from feeling unloved. "Such children may exaggerate their accomplishments to seem special—and may demand special treatment accordingly. Underneath it all, however, they still feel a sense of inadequacy, even shame, which they cover over with narcissistic pride."

As with the vexer, trying to find a connecting point through shared stories and experiences can help break down some of the barriers that separate the prima donna from others. It also helps to examine how the group welcomes her and how it may unintentionally exclude her. Sometimes, just feeling part of the team will help a prima donna let go of an excessive focus on herself.

"Burnout is the result of unrealistic expectations of self rather than the amount of work. Unrealistic expectations, if linked with one's personal worth, can destroy a person."

— LOUGHLAN SOFIELD AND CARROLL JULIANO

---

6. The burnout. "Bored people are boring." A colleague of mine once made this observation to describe both the cause and effect of burnout. Taken to extremes, burnout causes us to become cynical and harsh, judgmental and hostile. We stop seeing the joy in our work and start resenting the people we are called to serve. We become the absolute antithesis of a caring minister.

In the Church, burnout often takes hold when we stop having a life. Every waking, breathing moment becomes associated with the parish. We have no outlets, no other interests, no topic of conversation except the Church and what is wrong with it.

One response to a burnt-out coworker is to challenge her to reexamine her situation and to help her look at possibilities for change. Sometimes it's as simple as retuning a job description; other times it leads to a radical change of environment or position. In Sofield and Juliano's words, burnouts need "peers who love them enough to confront them...about their self-destructive behavior."

7. The seether. Extreme cases of burnout lead a person to a boiling point that seethes with hostility. This does not equate with anger as a response to frustration or injustice. Hostility sets up others as enemies and distorts one's view of the world. It's no wonder we instinctively try to get as far away as possible from such a person.

If my own efforts to deal directly with a seether are thwarted, it may require a conversation with her supervisor. I say this with some hesitation because there is far too much "triangling" going on in parishes today. This will be discussed at greater length in Chapter 9 as part of an examination of conflict. Nevertheless, there are times in which coworkers need some compassionate counseling and confrontation in order to help them face their own behavior and the effect it is having on others.

8. The victim. Eeyore, the sad-eyed donkey from the *Winnie the Pooh* stories, is a classic victim. His doom-and-gloom attitude colors his outlook and affects his interaction with others. Victims tend to feel as if everything is out of their control and are apt to name other people or circumstances as the cause of their woes and failings.

The work being done in support groups with victims of violence, addiction, and trauma generally involves positive reinforcement and empowerment. Some of us are overwhelmed by our responsibilities and the unending human needs connected to them. Rather than telling such a person to "get over it," we need to help them see their way through difficult situations with some concrete, "baby-step" solutions that help restore their self-confidence.

9. The kid. "He is in a state of arrested adolescence," a friend once lamented as she told me of her struggles in working with another staff member. She went on to elaborate: the inappropriate behavior at meetings and parish events; the lack of follow-through on important tasks; the clowning around when serious subjects need to be discussed. Such behavior is indicative of people who are too immature to be in parish ministry.

Often these are people with great big hearts who may have potential to be wonderful ministers. They need good mentoring, positive feedback, and adequate supervision. Gentle confrontation that helps correct behavior but doesn't squelch the spirit is crucial.

10. The hypocrite. This is a harsh term that describes the kind of people who test our faith most severely. They undermine the work of ministry by behaving in ways that violate the heart of the gospel. In the worst cases, they operate in unethical ways and abuse their positions—as pastors and priests, parish leaders, professional ministers, influential parishioners—in ways that are ultimately destructive to the community.

It takes a great deal of discernment to know how to respond to such situations. Efforts to confront them directly can be dangerous to one's own well-being. It might require approaching a supervisor—a staff member, pastor, bishop—in order to voice concerns about a coworker whose professional and ethical conduct is jeopardizing the well-being of the parish. This must be done with care in order to avoid becoming slanderous.

Situations like this wreak havoc in parishes, schools, and dioceses at large. Far too often, unrestrained gossip, conjecture, and infighting exacerbate the problem. As the Church continues to work on ways to deal with ethical misconduct, many dioceses are developing extensive systems for arbitration and accountability. If you are in a situation that compromises your own sense of justice, it is important to check out the appropriate venues for airing these concerns and then act accordingly.

Moving out of the bell tower

If there is one thing I wish I had known when I first started parish ministry, it was how to work well with others. Nothing has cost me more time or grief than being part of a fractious group or working alongside a difficult person. I know I "moved to the bell tower" in a figurative sense more than once as a way to cope with these situations. Keeping myself isolated rarely helped.

At a workshop on Ignatian spirituality, I heard the case for working well with others described succinctly by Joseph Tetlow, SJ. I thank him for permission to quote his words. He said:

Because we are all created in the likeness of a God who is Three Persons, we must understand that, in our turn, we are a person only in relationships. When I am on a team with another, I am not free to remain un-related. The only issue is how I will choose to relate: whether well or badly, creatively or destructively, and of course, in a holy or an unholy way.

CHAPTER 7

Volunteers

"I need someone...Anyone...??"

Picture this

Wendy is beginning to panic. The P-8 religious education program is scheduled to start in less than two weeks, and she is still short a fifth-grade teacher. Why is it she has no problem filling the positions for younger grades? Thank heavens for the parents who stepped forward at the last minute for grades 6-8. No one, so far, has volunteered to take grade five. How hard could working with twenty-five eleven-year-olds be?

Her plea from the pulpit at the weekend liturgies resulted in a few expressions of sympathy. Her hopes were raised slightly after the 9:30 Mass when one man approached her. "You looked so desperate," he said, "and I felt so sorry for you. It's a real shame that more people aren't willing to get involved." He then wished her well and went on his way.

She is now down to making phone calls. After being greeted by a variety of recorded messages, it is a relief to hear a live voice at the other end of the line. She didn't know Laura very well, only enough to say hello occasionally when she saw her cleaning up after coffee and doughnuts. She knew Laura had two teenage sons, and the youth ministry director described her as reliable.

Wendy explains the situation and Laura listens quietly. When she does speak, it is to voice her concern about having no prior teaching experience. "That's no problem," Wendy assures her. "I have all the books and materials you will need. I hope you can help me out. You're the last one on my list."

The following weekend it is announced that, if no one comes forward to teach fifth grade, the class will be cancelled.

Your thoughts

? What went wrong?

? What advice would you give Wendy about her recruitment strategies?

? How do you think the following people reacted to Wendy's dilemma? Laura? The fifth-grade students? The parents of the fifth-grade students?

? What other solutions could Wendy try to fill the fifth-grade catechist position?

A real-life scenario

For a couple of years, I volunteered for the Colorado Historical Society (CHS). As part of their speaker's bureau, I offered slide presentations, put together by other volunteers in the organization, on different aspects of Colorado history. At one point, I received a phone call asking if I would volunteer, as part of the CHS contingent, to help the local public television station's annual telethon. It intrigued me—a group of volunteers tapped to offer their services by a second non-profit organization. A few days before the telethon

I received another phone call. It was someone from the PBS station confirming my commitment and restating the date, place, and length of time involved.

When I arrived at the station, I was introduced to the other volunteers, given a CHS T-shirt, and invited to help myself to refreshments. A brief training period followed, during which we were taught to work the phones and enter donor data into a computer. While taking calls, two PBS workers were on hand to answer questions and troubleshoot problems. During the break, we enjoyed a full lunch.

Three days after the event I received a handwritten thank-you note from the volunteer coordinator at CHS.

> ► What's right about this scenario?

Blessing or burden?

Without volunteers, parish programs would shut down. Indeed, the very mission of the Church would be compromised. Volunteers do much more than "help out." They put their faith into action. Pastoral leaders have a critical role to play in facilitating this process. It's a delicate and time-consuming task. It's also exhausting.

There were times in years past that I longed to be freed from the responsibility of finding, training, and supporting volunteers. The work is extensive and, because it has to do with people, is in constant flux. There are numerous resources on the subject of volunteer management, and I wouldn't presume to think I could summarize them in a single chapter. What I will attempt is to offer some ideas and experiences that have been helpful to me, especially as they apply to a parish.

When planning for volunteers, I start with three basic questions:

> ► Who do I need?

> ► What will they do?

> ► When will they start?

After these are answered, I find the fourth question—how do I get them?—easier to tackle. Let's break this out.

In the first scenario, Wendy knew who she needed—or did she? Naming the job isn't the same as naming the person. This isn't about finding someone specific—that comes later. It's about identifying the type of person who has not only specific skills but also particular qualities that will match him or her to the job. Like Wendy, I all too often got desperate enough to search for a "warm body." It rarely worked out well, leaving both the volunteer and me frustrated.

Wendy would be better advised to paint a picture of someone who would work well as a fifth-grade catechist vs. casting a wide net and hoping someone—anyone—would jump in. Having a picture like this in front of her, Wendy could then help Laura discern whether the role of a catechist was something for which she was suited.

Portrait of a fifth-grade catechist

SKILLS AND ABILITIES
Able to communicate with children • Able to plan and organize • Able to carry out learning objectives • Able to use resource materials for both student and teacher

MOTIVATION
Desire to help children grow in faith • Desire to keep learning about one's own faith • Love for the Church • Love for children • Enthusiasm for the catechetical process • Willing to grow in knowledge and understanding about the Catholic faith

CAPABLE OF
Having fun • Being flexible (kids are unpredictable) • Generating creative ideas and activities to keep class engaged • Making a long-range commitment to planning, teaching, training, and enrichment

Most volunteer management systems call for creating job descriptions. This is helpful for work that is quite involved. A detailed job description can also be overwhelming. Keep it simple, direct, and honest—none of that "and other work as determined by..." stuff! The basic elements of a job description are:

▶ Job title

▶ Desired commitment

▶ Duties

▶ Desired qualities

▶ Accountability

▶ What to expect from the parish

Moving forward by planning backward

Over the years, I learned to work backwards in order to develop realistic timelines and not let critical pieces fall through any cracks. Here is how this looks:

I need a volunteer ready to start by _____ .

In order to meet this deadline, training/enrichment must be completed by _____ .

In order to meet this deadline, I need to confirm commitments and send follow-up information by _____ .

In order to explain responsibilities, answer questions, and surface expectations, interviews must take place by _____ .

In order to have volunteers contacted, confirmed, trained, and ready to start, I need to begin recruitment by _____ and end by _____ .

In the parish scenario, the only date Wendy seemed sure of was the first one. Getting backed into a timing corner precluded any of the preliminary conversations and catechist training that is essential to quality religious education. Allowing plenty of lead-time in the process is crucial to securing the very best volunteers.

Look ahead—way ahead—and anticipate needs for volunteers at the earliest stages of planning. It is helpful to keep an ongoing list of those who might be willing to help out. Attend newcomers' events and visit with people after Masses. Knowing parishioners now is one of the most effective ways to find volunteers later.

It's also a good idea to create contingency plans in case volunteers move or experience other changes in their lives. These might include:

► partnering more experienced volunteers with new or temporary ones;

► breaking one big job down into two or three more manageable/less demanding ones;

► realigning the schedule to allow more options for potential helpers;

► combining or bunching tasks to utilize the work of current volunteers;

► approaching other parish groups, such as the Knights of Columbus or those organized for women, singles, or seniors.

Now let's look at techniques that work and ones that fail, so that you can recruit volunteers without looking pathetic.

Five recruitment techniques that work

1. Be personal. The most effective way to recruit someone is one-to-one contact. Try to name a specific trait or talent that will go well with the position. This might be someone's knack for organization that suits her for committee work, or another person's sense of fun that makes him a natural fit for a social project. Help them "see" themselves in the role.

2. Be sensitive. For some people, the timing or circumstances of their lives make saying yes to a commitment difficult if not impossible. Be willing to take no for an answer, and resist the temptation to apply pressure. When someone is reticent to commit to a larger job, he or she might be willing to look at something less demanding. Offer alternatives, if this appears to be the case. In all circumstances, remember to thank the person for considering the request.

3. Be creative. Parish publications can be notorious for their dry, boring, and uninspired messages. Here's a different way to ask for a youth ministry volunteer:

> *The media tells teens to do it if it feels good. Their friends tell them to just do it. Who's telling them they're loved? Who's helping them choose Christ as their friend? Will you walk with our youth to help them choose Christ? We'll help you take the first step.*

Announcements, articles, and other promotional materials need to be invitational, intriguing, and engaging. Don't feel creative? Here's a job for another volunteer! Look for someone with professional marketing skills; they're often happy to lend their talents to such a project because the parish bulletin drives them crazy!

4. Be honest. Have you ever gotten yourself into a commitment and found it to be way more than you bargained for? It's important to be truthful with people and not promise what can't be delivered: a project's completion in an unrealistic period of time; the help of people who have not yet been recruited; the absence of meetings. Potential volunteers need complete and essential information to make wise decisions. Honesty up front saves time down the road because you won't have to look for someone else when the first volunteers fizzle out.

5. Be exact. Wendy's vague promise to Laura about giving her "books and materials" did not come close to defining a catechist's responsibilities. People are often more willing to consider something if they are given a good understanding of what the work will entail, for how long, and who will benefit from their efforts.

Techniques that fail

1. Begging. Wendy's desperate approach had a counter effect on the parishioners. Rather than creating a draw for potential candidates, her pulpit pleas may have conveyed a message that the catechetical program was a failure. Looking pathetic is not enticing.

2. Guilt trips. "If you love Jesus and Mary, you'll sign up to help..." The late Fr. Jim Dunning used this technique at catechumenate workshops to "motivate" participants to sign up for various tasks. It always brought a big laugh, perhaps because, as an audience of pastoral leaders, we knew this was an all-too-common recruitment method in our own parishes. Whether we're this blatant about it or not, guilt messages are quickly perceived as manipulative. Those who do respond out of guilt usually aren't very motivated and often end up making promises that are half-hearted.

3. Blackmail. Some ministers tack demands to their programs that require involvement, such as a certain number of volunteer hours "donated" by a parent in order for his or her child to participate in a youth event. Not only does this end up punishing the participant, but it also puts people on the spot. What if a job or home care situation precludes a parent's involvement? It's a risky proposition that may cause unintended embarrassment for families. If parental involvement is a goal, it's better to work with the appropriate planning groups to find other ways to invite participation

4. I'm only going to say this once. The hectic and mobile lifestyle of our society means that it may take three or four weekends before the entire community has "heard" an announcement. A variety of recruitment approaches are needed, and they need to be implemented over a period of time. Marketing experts tell us that the average person needs to hear/see something six times before it sinks in.

5. Threats. Wendy's last-ditch effort to find a catechist came across as a threat, one that implied the fifth-grade class wasn't worth the effort of looking for alternative solutions to the problem. Strong-arming people into involvement is disrespectful and counterproductive.

Follow-up

Once volunteers say yes, it is vital to follow up with some immediate and short-range items:

1. Confirmation. "I offered to help and no one contacted me." Does this sound familiar? The greater the lag between sign-up and follow-up, the more likely the potential volunteer will lose interest. A simple postcard, email, or text message, thanking the person for their promised involvement, is an ideal way to follow through quickly, easily, and efficiently.

2. Conversation. Whether or not an initial interview has taken place, it is still important to continue the conversation with the volunteer to find out:

▶ Who exactly is this person? What are his/her interests, skills, abilities, and gifts? Am I sure the volunteer is well-matched for this position?

▶ What amount of time is the volunteer able to give? Is she or he clear about what the job will entail? What will I need to do to accommodate the volunteer's schedule?

▶ What are the expectations of me and/or the parish? What do I need to tell the volunteer about the program, the committee, the event, or the ministry?

▶ How does the volunteer prefer to be contacted about last-minute changes and information?

▶ How can the volunteer contact me if he or she has questions, concerns, or needs?

3. Information. It's a frustrating experience to sign up for something and then not be given the pertinent "now what?" information. Generally the volunteer needs to know the "next steps": upcoming meetings and other pertinent events and dates; where, when, and how to obtain materials or resources; names and phone numbers of coworkers—committee heads, assistants, etc.; revised job descriptions; and any preliminary reading matter that will help familiarize them with their work.

Helping volunteers recognize their gifts

When I served as parish life coordinator for Pax Christi, I worked with the finance committee to foster a better understanding of stewardship within the parish. As part of this effort, the committee chairperson invited the business administrator from a neighboring evangelical church to speak at one of our meetings. The church was well-known for the high level of involvement among its members. In the course of her presentation, the business administrator described how their people were invited to participate. New members were asked to take part in a "know your gifts" workshop, offered on a monthly basis by a member of the staff. Intrigued, I asked if I could attend to see if it might serve as a model for our parish.

Entitled "Discovering my S.H.A.P.E. for Ministry," the two-hour session focused on topics such as Spiritual gifts, Heart's desires, Abilities, Personality, and Experience. (The S.H.A.P.E. format was first developed by Dr. Rick Warren, author of *The Purpose-Driven Life* and pastor of Saddleback Church, Mission Viejo, CA. Cherry Hills Community Church, Highlands Ranch, Colorado, adapted it for the gifts workshop discussed here.) Exercises included a spiritual gifts inventory, an interest finder, an abilities checklist, Myers-Briggs personality activities, and a reflection on past ministerial experiences. I was intrigued by the fact that there was no attempt to recruit anyone for ministry as part of the session. Instead, participants were encouraged to reflect upon their gifts and to prayerfully consider how they might best be used. It was clear that the Church was just one venue among many for this.

A few years ago, I worked as a consultant for an architectural firm that specialized in building and renovating churches. The head of the company told me of his frustration in designing and constructing multi-million-dollar facilities for parishes only to discover that they had put no thought into the potential use of their new space. It was like pouring stale wine into fresh wineskins. My services provided a way to incorporate ministerial planning into the overall project.

In one parish, I offered a presentation on stewardship and stressed that the donation of time and talent was just as vital as that of treasure. One older woman in the back of the room tentatively raised her hand and asked, "How do I know what my talents are?" It threw me for a moment, and I realized I had, all along, assumed that everyone knew what gifts they possessed. Coming to recognize this as a false assumption exposed major gaps in my thinking about volunteerism.

Too many of us have memories of negative work experiences, some of which stemmed from being placed in positions that didn't jibe with what we did well. As "managers," pastoral leaders have a responsibility to help volunteers succeed. This involves helping them name and affirm their gifts, matching talents and abilities with the right job, offering encouragement and feedback, providing training and information, and extending opportunities to "advance" as desired.

It is also essential not to squander or disregard the gifts that people have to offer. Unfortunately, this happens far too often. Volunteers who donated years' worth of work are suddenly told they are no longer needed. Ideas are discounted and past progress is ignored by new leaders eager to implement their own plans. It all leads to hurt and frustration and, in the worst-case scenarios, a withdrawal from the life of the community.

Time, the overlooked "t" in the stewardship formula, is precious. The time volunteers donate to their faith communities is something to be respected and valued. We can do this by eliminating unnecessary meetings and making the most of the ones we do have. Start and end punctually. Keep the work well defined and the expectations clear. Seize every opportunity to nurture volunteers, and be mindful of eliminating careless practices, attitudes, and behaviors that drive them away.

Now that I have them, how do I keep them?

Several years ago, after moving to a new town, I decided to try and meet new people through volunteering at a large and beautiful arboretum. I responded to a request for help in the gift shop during a special spring event that was sure to draw hundreds of visitors. When I arrived, no one was there to greet me or show me what to do. I soon discovered that there were other new volunteers present and that, together, we outnumbered the customers. The two senior volunteers made it quite clear that they were the only ones who could ring up sales and deal with clientele. I spent my time straightening up the merchandise and trying to look busy. After enduring a long and tedious afternoon, I left an hour early. I never went back.

Signing people up is one part of the volunteer equation. Retaining them is another. Parish work depends so heavily on their participation that having one dependable and hardworking volunteer quit can be a major setback. A certain amount of attrition is inevitable in any institution. It's also desirable. Nevertheless, it pays to be attentive to the reasons why someone chooses to leave before his or her time is officially "up." Let's look at why volunteers quit.

1. They don't see any value in their work. My experience at the arboretum was made all the more frustrating by the fact that it took me an hour to drive there and another hour to get back home. I expected to have my interpersonal skills and management ability put to good use. Instead, I spent the afternoon trying to find something to do. There was no clear reason for me to be there. I concluded that donating all of that time to an overstaffed and poorly managed organization was a waste.

2. They aren't challenged. This same experience turned out to be immensely boring. New volunteers are often not entrusted with enough challenge to hold their interest. It becomes deadly when that same person runs into others who actually stifle their attempts to help. As pastoral ministers we may rightly want to create a positive experience for new people by not overloading them on the first go-round. When we make the work too easy, however, we risk losing those who are fresh and eager to share their creativity.

3. They aren't sufficiently prepared. In our earlier scenario, we saw how quickly Wendy dismissed Laura's reticence about teaching. Putting a manual in someone's hands is not appropriate preparation, particularly for a ministry as important as catechesis. On the other hand, my personal experience at the PBS telethon put me at ease with the task at hand. We were given a sufficient amount of time to become familiar with our equipment, and having more knowledgeable people available to answer questions was reassuring.

4. They don't receive feedback. One frustrated pastoral council member shared his reason for stepping away from the position. "I went to meeting after meeting but never quite knew whether we were on the right track. The pastor is a very quiet man, and it was hard to tell if he approved of the direction we were taking. I finally just gave up." Lack of evaluation and feedback is a frequent complaint of parish volunteers. Very few people these days seem to have excess time to attend meetings that, like this pastoral council, appear to be nonproductive. Providing feedback on a person's performance or on the progress of a program or ministry helps volunteers determine the value of their commitment.

5. They got more than they bargained for. Being told a volunteer commitment only entails a "couple of meetings" and then finding oneself camped out at the church can drive away even the most dedicated helper. Unpleasant surprises also surface when volunteers find themselves paying for supplies or refreshments out of their own pockets, providing the food for their own affirmation events, or being left without adequate assistance or resources. Honesty and directness early in the recruitment process prevent hurt and resentment later on.

"No task is more important than the people involved."

— EMILY KITTLE MORRISON

What motivates volunteers?

Marlene Wilson, one of the country's foremost experts on volunteer management, identifies three primary styles of motivation:

1. Achievement. People motivated by this style want to see concrete signs of what their work is accomplishing. They're the ones who love placing thermometers in the vestibule to track donations to the parish building fund. Feedback and specific goals are important to them. They like solving problems and being left to work on their own. Christopher Weber, in his book, *Jesus-Style Recruiting* (Alpharatta: Visual Dynamics Publishing, 2011), cautions against going overboard on affirmation without also offering constructive praise. Such feedback, he says, "not only builds up your volunteer, but it also builds up their knowledge of the greater purpose, and advances the mission of your parish."

2. Affiliation. People motivated by this style are the first ones to RSVP for an appreciation dinner. They stay long after a meeting to visit. Socialization is one of the primary reasons for signing up, and they are drawn to group projects and teamwork. Having a personal relationship with their supervisor and making friends draws them to volunteerism.

3. Power. People motivated by this style want to impact and influence others. They are often "big picture" people, able to see the larger needs of the organization, and often gravitate to pastoral councils or other leadership groups. They are responsive to titles and positions of authority and credibility. Such workers are great self-starters and like persuading others to buy into institutional goals and objectives.

Based on my own experience, I will add a fourth style to the mix:

4. Education. While volunteering for the Colorado Historical Society, I found the range of interests among my fellow volunteers inspiring. One woman told me that, in addition to CHS, she also offered her time as a docent at both the Museum of Nature and History and the Denver Art Museum. A big draw for her was the opportunity to take part in the training that was offered in all three places. In like manner, volunteers in parishes are eager to offer their time and talent in order to grow spiritually and to learn more about the teachings and practice of the Church. The educational and formational processes attached to many youth, catechetical, and liturgical ministries are drawing cards for participation.

Name your style

Go over the four motivational styles, and pick out the one that most accurately describes you. Then consider the ways in which you generally choose to affirm and acknowledge volunteers.

- Are these usually based on your preferred motivational style?

- How might you stretch that method in different directions?

Twelve ways to care for volunteers

Here's a quick list of ideas to motivate, affirm, and acknowledge the work of volunteers.

1. Personalized notes. As a parish life coordinator, I used to write a weekly note thanking one of the parishioners for a specific act of generosity. When I left my position, one man sent me a letter telling me how much those notes meant. "They always came when I most needed them," he said.

2. Pass it on. When someone's work, abilities, or style is complimented, let them know!

3. Certificates with style. Desktop publishing programs make these easy to personalize—naming tasks or dates of involvement, accomplishments, and who benefited from the volunteer's efforts.

4. Perks. One parish names a volunteer of the month and awards them a close-in, reserved parking space for the entire month. This is especially cherished on Christmas or Easter. This may go to an individual, a couple, or an entire family.

5. Beauty spots. I know a DRE who plants a catechist garden each spring, one flower for each catechist and aide in the parish. Its loveliness graces the grounds throughout the summer and offers a visual reminder of the dedication of this group.

6. Promotions. Remember those power people? Giving them an opportunity to take on more responsibility is actually a reward for them. Public acknowledgment of this is even better!

7. Education. As mentioned earlier, many people see training and education as a benefit rather than a burden. Put energy into the planning of such programs by pulling together a variety of interesting and engaging speakers, topics, and resources. This lets volunteers know we think they deserve the best.

8. Celebrations. Every parish has at least one social maven, someone who revels in planning great parties. I always try to find these people and enlist their help for volunteer appreciation events. They are never at a loss for great themes, food, and activity ideas.

9. What do you think? A volunteer in a program or ministry quite naturally has the capacity to serve as an advisor or consultant, having acquired an insider's understanding of the parish. Providing venues for critique, evaluation, feedback, and suggestions tells them we hold their ideas and expertise in high regard.

10. The personal touch. Every volunteer has a life outside of the parish. When we are sensitive to the challenges they face and the demands on their time and energy, we show our regard for them as human beings. Track with their joys and sorrows by celebrating and remembering birthdays and special events.

11. Lavish communication. Being the last to know is a surprise most of us can do without. Making sure volunteers are "in the loop" is a vital and ongoing task of pastoral leaders. Happily, we have all sorts of technological help in doing this. Email, voice mail, text messaging, and blurbs on social networking are quick and easy ways to pass on important, up-to-the-minute information. Other thoughts on communication can be found in Chapter 8.

12. Feed the soul. It is pretty safe to assume that most volunteers in a parish want to grow spiritually in some way. Offering times and resources for prayer, retreat, and reflection not only helps them in this way but also underscores our primary mission as a faith community.

Volunteering for the whole family

With erratic schedules in many homes, parents often look for ways to spend additional time with their children. Volunteering as a family can strengthen relationships and bring faith to life. Parents appreciate not having to drag their children to church, and kids like being given responsibility and something interesting to do. Potential areas for family involvement include:

- ▶ Social outreach projects—making and serving meals, collecting clothing, distributing goodie baskets;

- Ushers and greeters—handing out bulletins and song books, taking up the collection, offering assistance;

- Parish social events—serving food, providing childcare, running festival booths;

- Religious education programs—teams of parent/teen or husband/wife catechists and/or aides;

- Readers—lectoring at Mass as husband/wife or parent/child combinations, reading special announcements or prayers;

- Liturgical environment—helping with design and creation of liturgical symbols and artwork;

- Music ministry—instrumental music provided by members of a family who rehearse and play together, adult-teen choirs and ensembles.

How do you stack up?

Assess your own approach to current and potential challenges in volunteer recruitment.

• I usually ask for volunteers in the following ways:

• I am successful _____ % of the time.

• I could also enlist the help of volunteers by:

• The groups of people I usually approach are:

• Other parish groups I might consider are:

I have great sympathy for the Wendys of the world. It's hard not to empathize with her frazzled nerves and desperate attempts to find a catechist at the last minute. I know just how she feels.

It also makes me grateful for the patience and grace that many volunteers have shown me as I have fumbled my way through ministerial planning. Many names and faces come back to me and help me embrace the work as one of blessing—rich, deep, and decidedly mixed.

CHAPTER 8

Communication

"Is that what I meant to say?"

Scenario

The staff gathered for its weekly meeting. One of the first things on the agenda was the revised procedure for reserving space in the parish complex. This issue had created several conflicts over the past few months, so the staff was eager to discuss it.

Bob, the business manager, handed out copies of procedural guidelines that included how to reserve a particular room, place an event on the calendar, secure keys, and communicate set-up needs. Clear and concise, these policies were meant to ease the process and thus minimize conflicts and cross-communications. Father Jim, the pastor, thanked Bob for his work and moved onto the next order of business.

At the conclusion of the meeting, Fr. Jim and Bob both retired to their offices, pleased at how well the meeting went. Harold, the head of maintenance, returned to his work satisfied that his role in setting up for meetings had been clarified. Joseph, the coordinator of youth ministry, rushed off to his next meeting, tossing the guidelines on his desk on the way out the door.

Dora, the DRE, felt upset and annoyed. Since she used the building extensively, it was disturbing not to be consulted about the procedures. Cynthia, the director of music, felt the same way. It seemed to be a "top-down" way of deciding things. Sue, the secretary, had mixed emotions. The new guidelines were bound to ease her work in managing the parish calendar, but she felt aggravated by the way it was handled. Will, the deacon, wondered why he, too, was left out of the loop when decisions were made about parish policies and procedures. After all, he had background as a business manager.

These four gathered in Dora's office where, behind closed doors, they vented their frustrations for the next two hours. They all felt as if their whole day had been ruined.

Your thoughts

?   How do you explain the various reactions among the different staff members?

?   Why were Dora, Sue, Cynthia, and Will so upset?

?   What did both Bob and Fr. Jim assume about the rest of the staff?

?   What is liable to happen to the new procedural guidelines?

A conflict in the making

After thirty-plus years of being in and working with ministry, I have reached a less-than-profound conclusion: It's not what we do in the Church that causes problems; it's *how we do it*.

Meetings like this tend to be the norm rather than the exception. On the surface, the issue is fairly benign. As discussed in Chapter 6, scheduling conflicts over space can be a major source of stress in parish work. Most of us would appreciate a clear and concise process to alleviate the problem.

The concern among the people huddled in Dora's office was, of course, not what was decided but how it was done. We can bet that, as that little confab continued, all sorts of past issues rose to the surface. It is a conflict in the making.

A major contributor to this scenario is a clash of communication styles. People are hurt and resentful because they feel overlooked. They weren't consulted and discussion was not encouraged. They felt "out of the loop." They weren't heard.

On the other hand, the disgruntled foursome didn't make their needs and perceptions known. Rather than ask for discussion time during the meeting itself, they waited until afterward and buzzed with one another. They weren't willing to speak up and express their feelings.

Over the years, I have worked as a group facilitator in several different parish and diocesan situations. In the process, I became sensitive to healthy and unhealthy communication patterns. I observed the way people tried—and failed—to be heard. I watched staffs and pastoral committees slowly deteriorate because they stifled their thoughts and emotions. Sometimes this happened because participants wanted to avoid conflict or they didn't think it was "nice" to contradict the pastor or someone else in authority. Other times they didn't want to prolong an otherwise tedious session with more discussion, or they thought their individual opinions didn't matter. And sometimes people just got too tired to keep a dialogue alive. It was easier to shut down.

Good communication is vital to the health of any institution. As Max De Pree puts it, communication "is the way people can bridge the gap..., stay in touch, build trust, ask for help, monitor performance, and share...vision." Communication entails expressing concerns and sharing ideas. It is also about listening and

Signposts of good communication

It's okay to talk.

It's okay to share feelings.

It's okay to tell the truth.

It's okay to disagree.

It's okay to ask questions.

It's okay to say no.

It's okay to challenge each other.

It's okay to laugh.

building relationships based on trust and understanding. Good communication is a give-and-take process requiring skill, ability, and commitment.

Male-female communication patterns

Several years ago, two sources of information came my way, almost simultaneously, that shed light on many of my questions about communications and conflict in parish work. One was the marvelous research of Deborah Tannen, a linguist, who has written extensively on the topic of how women and men communicate. At a time when the "men-are-from-Mars-women-are-from-Venus" phenomenon was starting to emerge as its own cottage industry, producing everything from calendars to cassettes, Tannen's work was refreshingly thoughtful. It was based on years of studying how people communicate in their homes and in their workplaces.

At the same time, a national organization for pastoral leaders released a study of parish ministries. Tucked into the middle of some interesting statistics was one that grabbed my attention: eighty-five percent of parish staffs are made up of women. While this wasn't exactly a radical revelation, seeing the actual number put things in perspective. The configuration in most parishes is a male pastor overseeing the work of several women. With this in mind, Tannen's work became even more exciting. I began to apply it to pastoral situations, and the results were extremely enlightening. One particular scenario stands out clearly.

I was asked to facilitate a visioning day for a parish staff. The DRE who contacted me mentioned that, much as the staff liked and respected the pastor, some of them felt that he wasn't hearing their ideas and concerns.

The day before our session a tragic incident took place in the parish. A deranged man entered the back of the church during Sunday morning liturgy, pulled out a knife, and began threatening to steal the collection. The ushers wrestled him into a small room where they kept him until help arrived. He became explosive when the police tried to remove him and was shot to death in the ensuing struggle. This happened during the communion rite.

The entire staff was understandably devastated by this incident and asked me to come as planned to help them sort out their feelings. As they began to speak, I noticed a distinct difference in their reactions, one that fell along gender lines. The three men, including the pastor, all began to talk about the sorry state of the culture and bemoaned a social structure that encouraged violence as a way to handle difficulties. The five women took the incident upon themselves in some way. The business manager lamented the fact that she hadn't developed better practices for securing the buildings. The musician wondered if she had seen the man in or near the church before. Each person cared deeply about what had happened. The men, however, tended to "globalize" the event, while the women "personalized" it.

Generalizations about males and females can be odious. Nevertheless, there is value in looking at speech patterns in a broad sense, keeping in mind that they can never apply to all men or all women. Tannen's work includes different conversational patterns employed by women and men. Four of these can be applied quite effectively to pastoral ministry

1. Report vs. rapport. In Anne Tyler's novel *Breathing Lessons*, there is a scene in which a middle-aged couple gets lost while driving to a wedding. They stop at a small country store for directions. The husband immediately takes out a map and works out their location with one of the locals. His wife, in the meantime, befriends the different people in the store and starts sharing the story behind their journey. Her means of seeking direction takes considerably longer than her husband's.

Men tend to view conversation as a way to exchange information. Their goal is to get to the point, the "bottom line," to focus just on the facts. Women use conversation to make connections. If there is a "bottom line," it is usually a dotted one.

This sheds light on one of the reasons behind the conflict in the opening scenario. Bob and Fr. Jim left the meeting satisfied because, in their minds, the situation was resolved. A plan was presented that was clear and to the point. The others, mostly women, had reactions that ranged from anger to feeling ill at ease because they expected more conversation about the matter. The staff may, in the end, have agreed with every aspect of the guidelines, but the process itself was the sticking point.

When I was in diocesan work, I wrote monthly progress reports and gave copies to the bishop, my department head, and my co-workers. The men were delighted with them and often complimented me on the "clarity" with which they were written. This was a remark I never heard from any of the female recipients. They preferred the "synthesis"—the way the reports meshed with aspects of their own work.

The pastoral ministry study cited earlier noted that women in ministry have higher expectations than men for consultative and collaborative relationships. This certainly affects their communication patterns. I have often heard women in ministry complain that their pastors don't listen to them. As I reflect on my experience with drafting the diocesan reports, I can see why the men were pleased with something that was written down in "clear and concise" fashion. It may not be entirely true that pastors—and other male figures—aren't listening. They simply may be more attentive to data than stories.

Women's rapport talk sometimes gives rise to unfair images of the "chatty female." One of the most interesting aspects of Tannen's research counters this stereotype. Women, she found, tend to speak up in public far less than men. This can be problematic when, like the women in the opening scenario, they hold back during meetings and then congregate afterward to buzz among themselves. They haven't spoken up in a place where they can be heard.

2. Dualistic vs. pluralistic. During my tenure as a diocesan director, the bishop and his staff engineered an extensive internal reorganization. This entailed a lot of meetings with diocesan personnel and clergy. By and large the men were delighted when a flow chart was eventually produced that showed the lines of authority and accountability. Most of the women viewed the same chart with negativity and skepticism. It represented to them a "set-in-stone" model that allowed for little flexibility and curtailed possibilities.

As men gravitate toward conversation that results in a decision, they appreciate either/or language. It is unambiguous, succinct, and leads to conclusive decisions. Women want to be consulted and also want to have options. They use both/and language. This is also the way convergent and divergent thinkers approach problems. Both styles are important in order to make sound decisions. Being aware of varying language patterns can help us ultimately reach consensus even if we approach it in different ways.

3. Compartmentalized vs. connected. In the opening scenario, Joseph is one character whose reactions remain a bit ambiguous. If the process bothers him, he doesn't show it. Instead, he tosses the guidelines on his desk and heads out the door to another meeting. We can presume that those papers will end up at the bottom of a pile somewhere and he won't give them another thought.

Men have a tendency to compartmentalize their lives and don't take things as personally as women do. Many times I have been part of a tense meeting where, as soon as it ends, the men start joking around or talking about sports. The women, in the meantime, either head for the door (and the "meeting after the meeting") or remain in place with their jaws tightly set.

This kind of behavior provides great fodder for comedians' routines about the lack of understanding between the sexes. Women see the past, present, and future flowing together like a river. They tend to make connections and expect the men around them to do the same. When those expectations aren't met, they can feel discounted and hurt. Men may then be left bewildered about what they said or did to trigger a negative reaction. Usually it turns out to be a matter of omission: they didn't make the connection.

4. Rules vs. guidelines. Communication patterns can be traced back to children and the way boys and girls learn to play. Deborah Tannen explains how this works in her book *You Just Don't Understand* (New York: Ballantine Books, 1990). "Boys' games have winners and losers and elaborate systems of rules that are frequently the subject of arguments....Girls, on the other hand, play in small groups or in pairs....Within the group, intimacy is key." Boys want to know where the power lies and what the rules and organizational structure are like. Girls tend to worry less about rules and will change the game, if need be, to make sure others are included or happy.

In the 1980s, the Vatican instructed the American Catholic bishops to reverse the then-current practice of preparing children for first Reconciliation after they had prepared for and celebrated first Eucharist. At the time, this news hit the catechetical leaders in my own diocese—a group composed primarily of women—hard. There were many reasons why they saw this as a poor practice, and their opposition to this mandate was fierce. The clergy, too, raised concerns about the issue but, for the most part, were willing to accept it and move on.

Our bishop suggested that, as a diocese, we take two years to study the sacrament and to usher in the changes in a gradual way.

The tone of the catechetical leaders changed overnight. All were happy with the idea. We ended up complying with the Vatican ruling as directed, but in the process also addressed deeper issues, particularly those having to do with adult participation. Thanks to our bishop's willingness to take it slowly rather than impose hard and fast rules, the transition happened in a peaceful fashion.

How to help your pastor (and everyone else) listen

Here are ten proactive ways you can help everyone you meet hear what you have to say:

1. Be direct—don't use go-betweens to carry messages for you.

2. Be courteous—don't interrupt.

3. Be timely—don't snag people on the run or wait to catch them off guard.

4. Be complete—follow the complete thought formula: I see... I think... I feel... and I want...

5. Be explicit—say what you mean and mean what you say.

6. Be up front—don't expect or assume that anyone else knows what you are thinking, feeling, needing, or wanting.

7. Be honest—don't think being "nice" equates with good communication.

8. Be respectful—avoid putdowns, gossip, sarcasm, and crudeness.

9. Be generous—embrace others' thoughts and ideas, and step away from always having the last word.

10. Be authentic—speak the truth with love

Conversational rituals

In her book *Talking from 9 to 5* (New York: Avon Books, 1994), Deborah Tannen examines the different linguistic patterns used in conversation that can cause misunderstanding. Although she focuses on the way women and men communicate differently, she also points out that gender is not the only issue. "Each individual has a unique style, influenced by a personal history of many influences such as geographic region, ethnicity, class, sexual orientation, occupation, religion, and age—as well as a unique personality and spirit." The following ten linguistic rituals can lend some insight into why our conversational paths may go off in different directions.

1. Saying I'm sorry when I'm not. I know a woman who punctuates almost every sentence with an apology. When I first met her, I was, at first, surprised by this habit and then became annoyed by it. Eventually I began to listen to what she was saying through her repeated use of "sorry."

For many people—women and men alike—saying "I'm sorry" isn't a literal apology. It is a ritual way of restoring balance to a conversation. In the case of my friend, it was her way of asking, "Am I taking up too much of your time? Are you interested in what I am saying?"

Ritual apologies work when both parties take them for what they are. When the hearer doesn't understand this, the apology sounds like the speaker is taking the blame for things that, in reality, aren't his fault. Such language can sound tentative, and it may be the reason some of us get talked into things we really don't want to do.

2. Taking blame. Have you ever found yourself apologizing for something for which you weren't responsible by saying, "I should have..."? This is another way of balancing conversation. It is done more often by those (especially women) who don't want to put someone else in a "one-down" position or who value rapport talk. When the hearer takes it literally—perhaps through responding,

"That's okay"—the speaker may feel unfairly "blamed" even though she initiated the thought.

On the other hand, many people (especially men) avoid blame even when something happened as a result of their actions. This can irritate those who are on the other end of the blame-assuming spectrum.

3. Giving criticism. I was once privy to a simple conversation that went like this:

> Joan (coordinator of religious education): "How did you think the children's Mass on Palm Sunday went?"

> Father Jeff (pastor): "We have to talk about doing this differently next year."

My own reaction to this brief exchange included an immediate sense of indignation on Joan's behalf. I saw Jeff's response as critical and harsh. Why, I wondered, didn't he temper his remark with a compliment?

I don't know how Joan felt about the conversation; she immediately moved on to something else. My own reaction set me thinking about how I give and receive criticism. Women tend to soften criticism in order to help others save face. While this may sound wonderfully compassionate and sensitive, it can also result in mixed messages—especially to those wanting explicit feedback. My own interpretation of Jeff's response as being too harsh would be viewed differently by someone who relishes an honest critique. They might see his answer as too vague rather than harsh.

4. Saying "thanks." After working on a joint event with a male colleague, I told him I thought it went well and thanked him. To my surprise—and annoyance—he responded by simply saying, "You're welcome."

This is a normal response, isn't it? It is when thanking someone is a way of expressing gratitude. When "thanks" is used ritually, however, it looks for another "thank you" to balance the conversation.

This may sound silly, but it does have an impact on relationships. Tannen points out, "Whenever something spoken automatically as part of a ritual does not receive the expected response, feelings can be hurt." By not thanking me in return, my colleague was, in essence, taking all of the credit for the success of our project. I was left feeling unappreciated for my efforts.

5. Ritual opposition. "I don't get it," a friend confided. "We all get along pretty well at my parish, but it seems like every committee involves someone who has to contest everything."

Tannen notes that males are more likely than females to use "'agonism'—a warlike, oppositional format—to accomplish a range of interactional goals that have nothing to do with fighting. Public debate is an example." This kind of talk can be taken as a personal attack by those who are not accustomed to it. For those uncomfortable with conflict, the "ritual fighter" creates an atmosphere at meetings that is close to unbearable. Recognizing this antagonism as ritual conversation may not alleviate all of the tension, but it can lessen it.

6. Asking for opinions. According to the pastoral ministry study, a greater number of women than men expect to be part of a ministerial team. Pastors, on the other hand, often make decisions to hire someone based on her or his ability to work autonomously. When a pastor or some other leader asks for an opinion, there is an assumption on the part of the team that one's recommendation will be acted upon. When this doesn't happen, there is disappointment and dejection. "What's the point?" they might say. "I'm not listened to, anyway."

Tannen says, "Many people ask those they work with for their opinions...to get a range of opinions, to make others feel involved, and to create the appearance, or the reality, of making decisions by consensus. But consensus does not mean (obviously, it can't mean) that all those who express opinions will get their way. It means only that everyone gets heard."

7. Business talk vs. personal talk. Many women mix business talk with conversation about their personal lives, and they may view women who don't do this as cold or aloof.

Men are more likely to mix business talk with banter about sports or politics and avoid bringing up their personal lives. We often regard the other gender's conversation as "small talk." This can create tension when we feel that what we say is considered trivial by our coworkers.

8. Giving praise. In the chapters on collaboration and coworkers, I placed a lot of emphasis on affirming and encouraging others. How this is done can take different forms. For those who use verbal praise, silence is a sign of disapproval. For those who don't use praise in the ritual fashion, saying nothing is a sign of the confidence they have in the other's abilities. It says, "I trust you enough to leave you on your own with this."

More women than men tend to want feedback about their work. Even so, formal performance reviews are the exception in parishes. Both women and men appreciate being praised for their work. Men, however, tend to interpret a lack of feedback as a sign that they are doing okay.

9. "Troubles talk." Tom, a male acquaintance, once told me about his frustration in getting together with his friend Gordon. "I enjoy talking to him," he said, "but every time I start to tell him about something I am struggling with, he tries to come up with a solution."

"Troubles talk" is a form of rapport that comes through commiseration. Tom doesn't want Gordon to fix his problem; he just wants him to listen. This kind of conversation may also be interpreted as complaining by those who don't engage in rapport talk. Thus, "troubles talkers" can be dismissed as chronic whiners or as having bad attitudes.

10. Humor. I once worked for a pastor with a very acerbic tongue. He used to poke fun continually at my programs or my decisions. I remember the surprise I felt when he would turn around and introduce me publicly with words of warm praise. I eventually learned to take his banter as a particular form of conversation and not a personal attack on my competence.

Men are more likely to use humor that is razzing, teasing, and directed at others. Women tend to use humor that is self-mocking. Women often mistake men's teasing as genuinely hostile, while men interpret women's humor as self-loathing. Each is likely to scoff at the other's form of humor.

Humor gone awry is a source of great tension between coworkers. With the heightening of awareness about sexual harassment, most workers are more conscious of how jokes and teasing can be misconstrued. If we feel humor is being used in ways that are destructive to our dignity, we owe it to ourselves and others to speak up.

Remember, as Emily Kittle Morrison puts it, "Communication is not a destiny—it is a journey."

"Listening is the heart of ministry. When we listen, we affirm and empower the other. Our listening is a gift to the other."

— LOUGHLAN SOFIELD, ROSINE HAMMETT, CARROLL JULIANO

The real key to communication

Ignatius of Loyola was considered an outstanding listener. It is said that he would refrain from speaking for several hours when attending a social function so that he could "know well" the people he was with.

I have a friend who is also a gifted listener. When you are with him, you know that his full attention is on you—not only on your words but also on your expressions and gestures. He asks questions to draw out further thoughts and often refers back to things you have told him before. Sometimes when you are talking, he will close his eyes, and you know he is shutting out other distractions in order to better hear what you are saying. It is not surprising that he is sought out as a confessor and spiritual counselor.

Improving our ability to communicate starts with a willingness to listen to others. It means paying attention, as my friend does, to the words and the meanings behind them. It means moving beyond stereotypes ("Just like a man." "Silly woman.") to understanding some of the patterns and rituals that are behind our speech. It means slowing down and recognizing the person in our midst as worthy of our respect and attention.

The way in which the staff in the opening scenario failed to communicate could very well lead up to a major conflict. It stands to reason that good communication can, in itself, be an inhibitor to conflict. It's one that has proven to be effective time and again. So let's listen up!

CHAPTER 9

Conflict

"Why can't we all just get along?"

Scenario

It wasn't often that Fr. Ed got a chance to eat with the rest of the staff in the office lunchroom. He was either caught up in meetings or away on sick calls. Sometimes he just couldn't emerge from the mountain of work on his desk. He joined Karen, the family life director, Sylvia, the coordinator of children's religious education, and Linda, the secretary, at the table and entered easily into their conversation. They were joined within a few minutes by two other staff members— Henry, the deacon, and Miriam, the receptionist. When John, the school principal, appeared without his lunch, Fr. Ed began to think something besides lunch was taking place.

At that moment, Karen abruptly shifted conversational gears by launching into a list of concerns about Sr. Janet, the director of faith formation. "She's abrupt and rude," she said, "and we find it very difficult to work with her." The others nodded in agreement, and each began to describe their own personal observations and encounters. "I hear that she's alienated a number of people in the parish," Linda said. "Someone told me they were withholding their donations to the collection until something is done about her." Sylvia went on to describe her own difficulties in having Sr. Janet as her supervisor. When Fr. Ed asked if she had made Sr. Janet aware of these problems, Sylvia slunk back. "She intimidates me. I find it way too difficult to talk to her."

As John began to talk about conflicts over the use of school facilities for religious education, Fr. Ed felt his lunch sitting like a stone in his stomach. His mind began to drift, and he wondered where the three other staff members were and if they even knew about this impromptu "meeting." He became increasingly uncomfortable with the situation and winced at the thought of Sr. Janet entering the room unexpectedly. This all felt extremely uncharitable.

He became aware that the group was awaiting a response from him. His frustration grew when his own efforts at getting beyond Sr. Janet to other potential sources of conflict were met with stony silence. "Something has to be done," Karen said with finality. It was clear that she—and everyone else—expected Fr. Ed to do it.

Your thoughts

? How would you feel if you were in Fr. Ed's position?

? What conflict(s) can you pick out in this scenario? Who do they involve? Can they be resolved?

? What factors are contributing to the escalation of the conflict with this staff?

? What can Fr. Ed do about this situation? What should he do?

Can anything good come out of conflict?

For five years my two children could barely make it through an afternoon without sniping at each other. During my years as a diocesan director, I spent at least one-third of my time dealing with conflict—between individuals, among groups, and within my own working relationships. I am very familiar with this topic.

Whenever there are two or more people trying to live, work, or play together, there is bound to be conflict. It is part of the development of any type of community. Scripture, of course, teems with such stories. Starting with Cain and Abel, the most brutal examples are among people who are closest to one another—family, friends, and fellow believers. Conflict is a normal aspect of genuine relationships.

This does not mean that it is always negative or destructive. As Charles Keating says, "The danger of viewing all conflict as unwelcome is that our fear might blind us to recognizing the usefulness of differences of opinion, the value of working through conflicting ideas to arrive at solutions or decisions that are more creative precisely because of the conflict. Differences, if not left unmanaged, can increase the group energy...heighten group innovativeness and actually lead to more effective problem solving."

The key word here is *manage*. While it is most desirable to resolve conflict, that may not always be possible. This is why Fr. Ed is suffering from heartburn. Managing conflict is a much more realistic goal. This entails being able to work together even though the source of our disagreement has not been resolved.

One of the greatest problems with unmanaged conflict is how easily it gets out of hand. Left unchecked it is not unlike those cartoons in which a dog and cat get into a fight, and, as they tumble around, everything in their path is sucked into the fray. The conflict becomes cyclic—coming round and round again to the same people and the same issues. It is also systemic, affecting everyone in the group in some way. Picture those Rube Goldberg contraptions in which one action sets off another and another and another. This is how it might look in a parish setting:

- ▶ The pastor refuses to allow the school principal to make a pulpit announcement about the upcoming "Back to School" night, thus affecting attendance.

- ▶ The principal changes the locks on the school office door, thus making the management of the Sunday morning religious education program more complicated for the DRE.

- ▶ The DRE schedules a family event, with lots of boisterous children, in a room adjoining the space where the youth director is trying to lead a high school prayer group.

- ▶ The youth director calls upon key office volunteers to help with a youth event the same day the secretary has to send out an all-parish mailing.

- ▶ The secretary pulls the business manager's announcement about the stewardship campaign out of the bulletin because it doesn't "fit."

- ▶ The business manager fails to send the pastor a critical piece of information after having a disagreement with him about staff salary guidelines.

As we can see, each person in this scenario may not get back directly at the one who crossed him or her. Instead, they react in some way—consciously or unconsciously—that affects someone else. The conflict becomes messier and more intense. It gets worse before it gets better.

There are all sorts of little ways conflicts are sparked. What turns them into raging infernos is the chemistry that sets off various reactions. Here are ten of the most common formulas for exacerbating conflict, along with their corresponding neutralizers.

1. Blaming. Did it strike you as unfair that Sr. Janet was, in absentia, assigned all of the responsibility for the friction among the staff? Scapegoating is a particularly odious way of escalating conflict. By projecting all of my problems onto someone else, I am safely off the hook. When I join forces with others to blame and complain, it becomes even easier to see one person or situation as the cause of every conceivable problem in the parish. Father Ed's fear that she might inadvertently walk in on this conversation was also tinged with aversion to the process. Ganging up on someone is profoundly unjust.

The antidote to blaming. We teach young children to use "I" messages as a primary way to avoid conflict. This simple technique works for all age groups as it allows us to name and own emotions without putting the responsibility for them on other people. (Unless, of course, we use such messages in the manner of the young boy who told his sister, "I feel like you're being a jerk.")

The more we let indignation and resentment grow, the more emotional we are likely to become. The higher the emotional levels, the more our judgment and perceptions become clouded. Parents defuse high emotional levels by requiring their young children to take timeouts. This isn't a bad idea for adults either. Writing down our thoughts in "I want, I need, I feel..." language can help with this as well.

2. Competing. Excessive competition aggravates conflict because we tend to perceive our goals as mutually exclusive. In the chapters on collaboration, coworkers, and communications, the need for support was reiterated over and over again. I have never come across a book on Christian ministry that advocated competition as a healthy practice. When our goal becomes to "one-up" each other, we become fractured and eventually isolated.

Competition may lead to manipulative or underhanded behavior that increases the friction between two people. These behaviors include persuasion (conning someone out of something), guilt trips, and manipulation.

The antidote to competing. The process of gift discernment, as noted in Chapter 6, can help counter this problem. When I name and embrace my own as well as another person's gifts, I have less of a need to compete. I am able to recognize that we both have something to contribute, each in our unique way. This allows me to be attentive to someone else's success rather than waiting (and hoping?) for evidence of their failure.

"Cooperation, the assumption of a win-win situation in which our goals are not mutually exclusive, allows us to manage conflict." — CHARLES KEATING

---

3. Sabotaging. I once worked with a parish secretary who pulled your announcements out of the bulletin if she was mad at you. She would also give callers vague and inaccurate information regarding your whereabouts. This kind of overt sabotage might be a bit over the top, but it does happen. More often, however, sabotage is carried out in covert ways, sometimes by the affable people described in Chapter 6. This behavior renders others powerless by withholding information or by using one's title, role, or resources to undermine someone else.

We may unwittingly sabotage another person's work or authority through a chronic need to "fix" things. This might be the pastor who sidelines the policies of a school, for example, by giving his tacit approval to a group of highly critical parents. By virtue of his position he can override the principal's authority and invite even greater tension.

The antidote to sabotaging. If we are especially trusting souls, we might be reticent to admit that we have been sabotaged. The first step in dealing with any conflict is to acknowledge it. Denial only leads to its acceleration. Naming the situation can then help us to discuss it with the responsible person. In some cases these people may be unaware of the way in which their actions undermined our plans and compromised our authority. In more severe cases, such as the behavior of the parish secretary, a confrontation is needed.

Sometimes people resort to sabotage when they feel left out. Maximizing the participation of coworkers and volunteers in decision making can help offset the tendency towards sabotage. Those involved in a plan are less likely to do something to make it fail.

4. Intimidating. In the opening scenario, Sylvia named something about Sr. Janet that may have been operative in the other staff members as well: She was intimidated by her. This could be due simply to clashing personality styles. It might connect to Sr. Janet's status as a woman religious, her title as "director," or her extensive experience as a minister. Whether she intends to intimidate is another question.

One common reaction to strong-willed or severe personalities is to avoid direct contact with them. There are some people we avoid because they seem somewhat dangerous. In the novel *Like Water for Chocolate*, they are described as having "frigid breath." They snuff out the fire within us through their overpowering ways.

The antidote to intimidating. When one goes into overload, it is easy to become abrupt. In order to collaborate, it is important to be acquainted with the tasks and responsibilities of our coworkers. This can help avert clashes through an increased sensitivity toward another's workload. Using "how can I help" language conveys a willingness to be supportive. Getting to know one another on a more personal level can also alleviate this situation. One way to do this is by arranging to have lunch or going for a walk together. When doing some kind of off-site activity, avoid church talk and try, instead, to find a personal connecting point.

5. Trivializing. It is a hurtful and damaging thing to infer that someone else's perceptions and feelings don't matter. One way this happens is through careless comments, such as, "Get over it," "What's the big deal?" or "You're making a mountain out of a molehill." Just as placing all the blame for a conflict on another person is an unhealthy way to deal with the situation, so too is shrugging it off as inconsequential.

Some people trivialize conflict by clowning around. While humor can be an effective way to defuse tension, some things are no laughing matter. This is especially true when coworkers express their needs, hurts, and fears.

The antidote to trivializing. One reason for trivializing a conflict is the inability to face it. Inappropriate humor is a way to suppress or deny that there is a problem. Attentiveness is a good antidote to this. Listen carefully to others and ask that they do the same for you. Be mindful of temptations to flee from a confrontation through making light of it.

6. Attacking. Father Ed's increasing agitation over the lunch-time gathering was well-founded. It came across as a personal attack on Sr. Janet, and he was right to see this as extremely unchar-itable. It was also an indirect attack on his leadership. There was some type of agreement among the staff that they would, together, approach him. The fact that the confrontation came as a surprise to him might mean that no one attempted to talk to him about the issue on a one-to-one basis. The meeting took place during his lunch hour, his free time. It is the kind of approach that puts some-one on the defensive.

In the heat of an argument or its smoldering aftermath, it is easy to confuse the person with the issue. Lashing out in anger only makes matters worse.

"The more threatening the initial attack, the more intense the reaction against it." — LOUGHLAN SOFIELD AND CARROLL JULIANO

The antidote to trivializing. Several years ago, Father Tom Downs, a kind and compassionate pastor, taught me an important lesson. We were co-facilitating a conflict-resolution session with a parish staff. There was a great deal of anger within the group, and those who did speak out tended to direct their ire at particular individuals. It seemed like we were spinning our wheels until, finally, Father Tom began to explain that anger was a secondary emotion, one that overlays the deeper emotions of hurt or fear. He then asked everyone to name her or his individual fears and hurts. There was a dramatic change in the room's atmosphere. Tension levels dropped and some poignant sharing began. One person described her fear of losing her job. Another one described his hurt at being excluded from decision making. Going below the surface of the anger moved the group from blaming others to naming issues.

7. Triangling. Sylvia illustrated perfectly what triangling is all about. Instead of talking to Sr. Janet herself, she went to a third person, presumably in the hope that he would take care of the situation. Those prone to "troubles talk" may seek out a third party just for the purpose of gaining an ally in the struggle. Neither behavior is particularly helpful.

The antidote to triangling. Be direct. If your problem is with someone else, talk to that person before things get out of hand. Since Sylvia was so intimidated by Sr. Janet, she might have gone to Fr. Ed for advice and insight. This employs the help of someone else, not for the purpose of recruitment, but for assistance in dealing appropriately with a difficult person.

Another reason that people triangle is because they are uncertain about what to do. After identifying the cause of a conflict, the second step in the management process is making a decision about how to address it. If approached as "third parties," we can encourage direct contact between the two people and then get out of the way. Being a go-between is for official negotiators.

8. Gossiping. Some of the most destructive behavior in parishes involves gossip and third-hand information. In the opening scenario, Linda uses it as a way to underscore the staff's case against Sr. Janet. Beware of sentences that start with phrases like, "I heard..." or "People are saying..." or "Word has it..." or "I just thought you should know..."

The antidote to gossiping. The antidote to this is simple: don't initiate, participate in, or pass on gossip. Nip a conversation in the bud when it heads in this direction. If you are in a position where you are a potential "ear" for gripes, such as a secretary or receptionist, devise a one-sentence response to cut the conversation off. Your callers will soon get the message.

9. Obfuscating. Being fired or "downsized" is a humiliating experience. I have heard more horror stories about parish "pink slips" than I care to remember. One woman received a message from her pastor on her answering machine. Another figured she had been let go when she saw an ad for her job in the parish bulletin. Still others received letters in their parish box or through the mail. The decision to let someone go without the proper amount of due process is bad enough. The indirect way in which the person is informed about the decision makes it even worse. The most extreme cases lead to full-scale battles, some of which even end up in court.

Confusing and indirect means of communicating with each other usually happens in much less dramatic ways. When the issue itself is clouded, it affects the overall picture and makes conflict management even trickier. Dragging in past history is another way to heighten the tension.

The antidote to obfuscating. The last chapter dealt with communication methods that help correct this kind of indirectness. After an argument, emotions are likely to be intense. Writing out what happened, how you reacted, and how you can respond is a calming and clarifying exercise

10. Sidelining. My daughter once told me that one thing she learned early about her father and me was that she couldn't bypass one of us to get her way. "You were a united front." It was a nice, affirming revelation, especially after years of feeling overwhelmed by the need to negotiate family disagreements.

Going over a supervisor's head—"straight to the top" (which usually means the pastor)—is a classic way to sideline a conflict. It muddles the lines of accountability and sets one against another. In the confusing aftermath, we get our own needs met while ignoring the concerns of others.

The reverse situation occurs when someone interferes with another's supervisory role. If Fr. Ed, for example, starts to act as Sylvia's supervisor, especially without Sr. Janet's knowledge, he will place himself in a triangling position and create further strain between these two women. It will eventually have a significant impact on the rest of the staff and on the parish catechetical programs.

The antidote to sidelining. Think "system." Who will be affected if I interfere in a conflict with someone else—by fixing, triangling, or usurping authority? The scenario in which one act of sabotage sets off others illustrates how the whole system is eventually affected.

Situational strategies

"ADAPT" to prevent conflict

Agree

Dodge

Adjust

Persist

Take in

Not every conflict can be resolved. Some of them don't need to be. We only have so much time and energy. This means figuring out which battles to pick, to let go of, to avoid, to negotiate, and to lose. We need to know when to ADAPT:

Agree—A "win-win" strategy is often regarded as the ideal way to manage conflict. It can be one that feels the best because everyone comes away satisfied with the outcomes. It is not the only way to deal with a conflict situation, but is a useful approach when an objective is to learn from the conflict or when we want to merge insights, gain commitment, or foster intimate relationships. The Sr. Janet–Sylvia situation is an example of how this strategy might overcome some of the "intimidation" issues without costing anyone their job or dignity.

Dodge—While agreement is seen as an ideal, avoidance is regarded as the ultimate taboo. This is valid when dodging a conflict involves denial, repression, or suppression. On the other hand, some fights just aren't worth the effort. The issue may be too trivial to warrant a lot of attention. There are some people whose clout is so much greater than mine, there is no way I can come out ahead. The damage done by the conflict might far outweigh the benefits. And sometimes others can solve problems better than I can.

Adjust—Conflicts over "liturgical correctness" illustrate when compromise might be the best solution. Cases in point are weddings and funerals. The issues involved—whether to play a certain song or read a certain prayer—are generally much more important to the couple or the family than they are to the minister. There are ways to compromise that won't jeopardize liturgical norms. Doing so is often the more pastoral choice.

Adjustment is also helpful when dealing with peers who have an equal amount of power and authority. It is needed in a mutual style of leadership. Reaching a compromise, even if it is less than perfect, can be an expedient course of action, particularly when groups are unable to reach consensus.

Persist—A harsh reality of life is that sometimes people lose. Remember the school principal I mentioned who once told me that, like it or not, she has to be a sovereign leader when it comes to fire drills? Emergencies call for quick and decisive action that can't be concerned with stepping on toes or hurting feelings. When an issue threatens the welfare of a group, persistence serves as a protective measure.

Take In—Accommodation is another perceived taboo in conflict management, especially for leaders. There are times, however, when this approach is necessary—especially when we realize we are wrong (it happens!) or when we are outmatched. This is also a helpful way to move forward when an issue is more important to someone else than it is to me. For those who are developing subordinates, accommodation allows for greater empowerment.

Four rules for fighting fairly

1. We find out the problem.

2. We attack the problem and not the person.

3. We listen to each other.

4. We care about each other's feelings.

(Source: Grace Contrino Abrams Peace Education Foundation, Inc.)

Words that hurt, words that heal

Conflict can actually be a positive experience when we interact without hostile confrontation, and remain non-defensive and non-judgmental. The language we use makes all the difference. Words have a great capacity to comfort, affirm, encourage, and heal. They can also do a great deal of harm. Consider the following story, paraphrased from Joseph Telushkin's book *Words that Hurt, Words that Heal* (New York: William Morrow and Company, 1996):

> There is a rabbinical story about a man in a small town who slanders the rabbi. He feels remorseful about his behavior and asks the rabbi for forgiveness, offering to make amends through undergoing a penance. The rabbi tells him to take a feather pillow, cut it open, and scatter the feathers to the wind. He should then return to see the rabbi.
>
> The man does as he is told, then comes back to the rabbi and asks if this is sufficient reparation. "Almost," the rabbi tells him. "Now you must go and collect all the feathers."
>
> "But that's impossible," the man protests. "They have been scattered all over the countryside by the wind."

"Precisely," the rabbi answers. "It will be as impossible to repair the damage done by your words as it is to recover the feathers."

Jewish teaching compares the tongue to an arrow. Once it unleashes harsh words, it cannot take them back. Lies, slander, gossip, rumors, and put-downs are examples of destructive language. So, too, are terms like "You should have…" or "We never do things that way…" One way to gauge the power of our words to hurt is by running what we have to say through three mental filters:

- ▶ Is it true?
- ▶ Is it necessary?
- ▶ Is it kind?

Words have an equal capacity to heal and to inspire. Therefore it is important to use language that is forgiving, compassionate, helpful, and fair. What we have to say may not always be easy. If we are to help others grow, we must be honest with them, something that requires tact and discretion. As Kaleel Jamison puts it, "It's not my goal to make other people comfortable. It is my goal to offer the kind of straight talk…that produces growth—and may bring with it temporary discomfort."

Forgiveness as a way of life

Several years ago I took part in a "Remembering Church" institute, sponsored by the North American Forum on the Catechumenate. The group consisted primarily of pastoral ministers and, as we worked through topics of alienation and forgiveness, the facilitator, Father Jim Dunning, made an insightful observation. "There is probably more collective hurt within this group than will ever be found in an average parish."

It was true. There were those who had known the humiliation and devastation of being fired without just cause. Others had put up with years on parish staffs in which feuding and bickering were relentless. Some felt hurt by the way the Church excludes women and married men from full participation in priestly ministry. And still others felt bone-weary after years of hard work and little or no acknowledgment for all they had contributed. The best antidote to being beaten up by conflict is forgiveness. This isn't easy, especially if we have suffered betrayal or savage criticism.

Someone once said that Cain will never stop killing Abel until he learns to find him in his own heart. We will never be able to eradicate all conflict, but we can learn to manage it. As we do, we can learn to stop hurting one another and, instead, find a place of understanding in our hearts.

CHAPTER 10

Care of the minister's soul

"How to get a life"

Scenario

As the last notes of the closing song sounded, Aidan's mind raced ahead to the next scene. The neophytes were gathering with family, friends, and the rest of the community for the reception in the parish hall. There were certificates to be handed out and pictures to be taken. If he hurried, he could make it up the side aisle and out of the church before the bulk of the crowd.

The Holy Saturday service had been beautiful, or so Aidan thought. He was so distracted by various details he missed most of it. He thought about borrowing the videotape filmed by one of the neophyte's spouses and at least viewing the initiation rites. As the last of the clean-up crew left, he made a final check of the building and then headed for his car. Letting out a deep sigh of relief, he congratulated himself for having made it through another Easter Vigil. As coordinator of the RCIA he knew that this night was supposed to be the high point of the whole process. Somehow, each year it turned into an endurance contest. He was generally so tired by the time the Easter bonfire was lit that he just looked forward to having it all over.

Maybe it would be different next year...

Your thoughts

?   What is the cause of Aidan's fatigue and distraction?

?   What would help him rectify the situation?

?   Can you relate to Aidan's experience? Are there events or moments you should be looking forward to but, instead, want to be over with?

?   How do you care for yourself as a minister?

What happened to my life?

Aidan joins the cast of other ministers in the scenarios we have examined:

1. Sister Mary Alice, burnt out over the lack of congruence between her gifts and the job.

2. Stan, frantically searching for the perfect time management system.

3. Lydia, deflated when her plans for adult education go awry.

4. Kevin, blindsided by the vigorous criticism about his liturgical decisions.

5. Rita, victim of cross-scheduling and suspicious of inner-office sabotage.

6. Steven, discouraged by the conflicts and power struggles on a fractious pastoral council.

7. Wendy, desperately seeking a fifth-grade catechist.

8. Dora and company, grousing behind closed doors about the way procedural guidelines were developed.

9. Father Ed, beleaguered by the criticisms of the staff over a coworker.

Notice the adjectives used to describe these people and their predicaments—burnt-out, frantic, deflated, blindsided, suspicious, discouraged, desperate, grousing, beleaguered. Aidan's situation is a sad outcome of all of this. He misses, via distraction, the most sacred and joyous liturgy of the entire year.

It took me far too many years to realize two essential realities about pastoral ministry:

▶ I need to have a life.

▶ No one else can or will make that happen for me.

Watercarriers of the community

Listen to these wise words by Ron Farr, from his article "Sabbath Resting in God" (*Weavings*, vol. VIII, no. 2):

> Christ calls each of us, laity and clergy alike, to find ways to minister to the brokenness of our workplaces, neighborhoods, or world. The more we enter into the hearts and dilemmas of others, the more suffering we uncover, and the more we are wounded by our own compassion for them... Yet, no matter how many hours of service we put in, still the undertow of ministry pulls us out into even deeper waters. We soon find ourselves struggling just to stay afloat in a turbulent ocean of human need that extends as far as the eye can see. All our efforts to minister to such colossal brokenness begin to feel like nothing more than a few drops in the bucket....We grow weary in the struggle.

My good friend Barbara Radtke has taught in ministerial programs for decades. In an e-mail, she described an experience of helping a group of students deal with a national crisis:

> The school asked us to take a portion of the class time to focus on the national situation. I had a graduate class in Christology, and all the people were ministry students. I identified them as caregivers in some way, and I asked them what advice they would give each other to take care of the caregivers. Very few could do it. They wanted to say what they would do for others but not how to take care of themselves. It ended up a very interesting discussion.

The *watercarrier* played a very important role in the tribal life of ancient cultures. Max De Pree likens this role to that of leaders:

> Watercarriers transfer the essence of the institution to new people who arrive to help us and, eventually, to replace us. They understand that resources can be nourished as well as managed. All of the visions, all of the strategies, all of the implementation, all of the day-to-day operations, are carried out by one potential watercarrier or another, always working in concert with, and in need of, other potential watercarriers.

Pastoral ministers are watercarriers. Through their planning, sharing, caring, organizing, explaining, teaching, rehearsing, presiding, facilitating, training, empowering, and delegating, they do indeed "transfer the essence" of the Church to others. It is challenging, exhausting, and often thankless work. Carrying the water of ministry takes dexterity and humor, creativity and compassion, persistence and faith.

What happens when the watercarrier gets thirsty? How will she or he find refreshment and rejuvenation? The "undertow" of ministry can be overpowering, and it is essential to take care of one's soul in order to survive. As Reverend Thomas Keating puts it, "The more difficult the ministry, the more a contemplative dimension is needed" (Contemplative Outreach Conference, Denver, CO. March, 2001).

Unfortunately, many of us either don't know how to incorporate this dimension into our lives, or we expect others to take care of it for us. We may put it off, awaiting the distant day in which we can find time for retreat or renewal. Like Aidan, we may have to resort to watching what we missed on videotape.

In his best-selling book *Care of the Soul: A Guide for Cultivating Depth and Sacredness in Everyday Life* (New York: HarperCollins, 1992), Thomas Moore describes loss of soul as "the great malady of the twentieth century." It is pretty safe to say this malady has followed us into the twenty-first century. Of all people who should understand this and thus live soul-full lives, it is pastoral ministers. Yet, as the earlier list of adjectives illustrates, far too few give adequate time and attention to their spiritual well-being.

Moore names an increase in "function" as a sign of soul-loss. When our lives become a list of to-do's or, like Aidan, "making it through" something, we are in a functioning mode. Gone is the beauty, the wonder, the appreciation. Gone is the joy of life itself.

What follows is a ten-point "plan" for ministerial self-care. It comes from my own experience of being on overload far too often and from the practices that eventually brought me back to life. It also comes from the wisdom of various individuals who have shown me what it means to be an authentic minister. It is certainly not an exhaustive plan, but it just might strike some chords in your own life.

Ten-point plan for staying refreshed and renewed

1. **Expand.** Can you name two new things you learned last year that were:

  ▶ connected to your ministry or role in the Church?

▸ connected to your life outside of your job/role?

There is a need to keep ourselves up-to-date as ministers through reading and study. Nevertheless, pragmatic concerns might cause us to neglect this area of our lives. Intellectual stimulation is tremendously inspiring and can fill us with renewed energy. Just consider the enthusiasm of coworkers who return from a seminar or workshop, fired up and eager to talk about new ideas.

"One thing life taught me—if you are interested, you never have to look for new interests. They come to you."

— ELEANOR ROOSEVELT

My experience of working with the juggler (see Chapter 2) is an example of learning something new that provided fresh insight into an old topic. In this case it was time management, and it quickly spread over into areas of spirituality.

There are a number of ways to expand intellectually:

Take a class. This doesn't have to be directly connected to ministry. Years ago, I received a freelance assignment to develop an educational workshop that included a PowerPoint presentation. Since this was a relatively new program at the time, I signed up for a one-day class. I came away with increased energy and new skills. I have since incorporated my husband's beautiful photographs into presentations that I offer, using PowerPoint. That single opportunity expanded into an entirely new way to carry out work that I love. With the plethora of new technologies available through the web, phone apps, and tablets, opportunities for expanding knowledge and skills are greater than ever. The possibilities are varied and exciting.

Read from a variety of sources. If you were given a $100 gift certificate to your favorite bookstore, what sort of purchases would you make? Would they all be from the same section of the store? I keep a running list of books in a pocket of my day planner. Whenever I read a review, see a reference, or otherwise hear about a good book, I write it down. Thus I have at my fingertips all sorts of options for spending that $100. Branching out in our selection of reading—from non-fiction to fiction, from books to periodicals—is another way to expand our reading habits.

Watch films, videos, and TV that feed the soul. There is a lot of well-deserved criticism directed at banal movies and vapid television programming. On the other hand, there are many fine productions that educate, inspire, and challenge. The practice of media awareness in our own lives can assist us in becoming more discriminating as viewers and consumers. Read reviews and talk to friends and colleagues to find out what you may be missing. With the availability of streaming films onto computers, the possibilities for finding such material is all the more exciting.

Expansion enables us to polish our gifts. It takes discipline to keep growing, to find the time to read, to study, to visit museums, to listen to good music, to appreciate history. Each activity helps to enlarge our capacity to understand, to think, and to imagine.

2. Connect. I read an article once that advised "quitting early." The writer's point was that we should extricate ourselves from our jobs so as not to make work the sum total of our lives. Parish ministry is so demanding that this recommendation may seem next to impossible. For clergy, of course, it is also not advisable! Nevertheless, becoming overly immersed in the parish "job"— whether that's pastor or lay minister—can be deadly to heart and soul. When we have a sense of connectedness with others, we are able to move beyond our immediate environment to something larger.

In order to assess your own need for making stronger connections, consider your answers to these questions: If I quit my job today, what would my social life look like? How about my intellectual life? my spiritual life? Making connections with others deepens our authenticity. Otherwise, we run the danger of taking up residence in an ivory tower. The following story, by Joann C. Jones, and paraphrased in Jack Canfield and Jacqueline Miller's *Heart at Work* (New York: McGraw-Hill, 1996), illustrates this point.

> A second-year nursing student recalls a class in which her professor administered a pop quiz. A good student, she breezed through all of the questions until she reached the last one. It left her puzzled. "What is the name of the woman who cleans the school?" Even though she had seen this woman on many occasions, she had to leave the question blank.
>
> At the end of the class another student asked if the last question would count towards his final score. "Absolutely," the professor replied. He reminded the class that, in their nursing careers, they would meet all sorts of people. "Each one is significant. Each one deserves your attention and care, even if it's just a simple hello."
>
> It was a lesson this young student never forgot.

We can only guess at the number of people Aidan rushed by in his efforts to "make it through" the Easter Vigil. Connecting with others increases our capacity for empathy and compassion. It helps us notice those around us. It reminds us that we all—doctor, patient, cleaning woman—have a name, a face, a story, and an intrinsic value. It reminds us to say hello.

3. Cherish. There is a television show that first came on the air in the early '90s. It proved to have enormous staying power. Reruns are shown at all times of the day and night, and the actors are still highly recognizable, even though some appear only sporadically in films and reality shows. The program's simple title explains its enduring popularity: *Friends.*

"My friend is one...who takes me for what I am."

— HENRY DAVID THOREAU

When on overload, it is time with family and friends that often suffers. Sometimes we feel so drained by a difficult coworker or stressful work environment that our energy is spent by the time we get home. Nevertheless, every truly effective minister I ever met is someone grounded in his or her relationships with family and friends. These relationships keep them genuine by restraining their tendencies toward self-centeredness, senseless ambition, and isolation.

When my son, Eric, was in high school, he jarred me out of such tendencies in a rather interesting way. I had just returned from a trip in which I gave talks to catechists and pastoral leaders around the country. As I was unpacking, he strolled into the room and asked what we were having for dinner. Cutting short my tirade about being tired and needing time to unwind, he looked at me with a wry smile and said, "You know, Mom, my job is to keep you humble." Indeed.

He reminded me of something vital. It was not that my sole value was as chef and valet. It was that I had a place in the family. Whether I cooked or ordered pizza, the need to have dinner—together—was important. I could jet all over the country talking about family, but my lived experience of it was what mattered most. It was a humbling thought.

Retired author and speaker Dolores Curran used to challenge her ministerial audiences about their propensity toward neglecting their own families as they poured energy into caring for others. It called into question, she said, whether we were raising a bunch of "apostolic orphans."

As one's attention to the family declines, so too does time spent with friends. Letting go of friendships out of neglect is akin to losing a treasured heirloom—it can never truly be replaced. I came across this wonderful bit of wisdom in the August 2001 issue of *O—The Oprah Magazine*: "There are two kinds of friends: friends of time and friends of like mind. The first...give our lives continuity; the second... give our lives possibility. Both stir our capacity to care and connect."

Email, text messaging, and social media all offer quick and convenient ways to stay connected with friends. We also need extended time with friends, though, in some type of face-to-face, voice-to-voice connection. Such encounters challenge and re-direct us, holding us to the truth of where we came from and who we are becoming.

4. Laugh a lot. It should be evident by now that I am in full agreement with Teresa of Avila when she counseled against humorless saints. Ministers who become "sour-faced" also become brittle. Their edges are sharp and people move away from them in order to avoid getting slashed to pieces. Too much responsibility—real or perceived—can make us this way. So, too, can a misplaced sense of holiness. Ronald Rolheiser says, "Sanctity is as much about having a mellow heart as it is about believing and doing the right things, as much about proper energy as about truth."

"From silly devotions and sour-faced saints, Lord, deliver us."

— TERESA OF AVILA

Humor is a great way to keep the heart mellow. The ability to laugh can carry us through a crisis or just a bad meeting. One can get an immediate feel for the health of a parish or diocesan environment by the presence or absence of laughter. Offices, committees, and meetings saturated with tension and infighting are generally devoid of any form of levity. This creates an ominous and heavy mood.

Being able to laugh improves working relationships and helps us manage our work more effectively. There are many health benefits to smiling and laughing. Remember the one essential requirement to being a juggler? It is the ability to forgive ourselves. This entails a healthy dose of humility and a large capacity for humor. When we take ourselves too seriously, we lose both of these elements. My son's reminder about his role in keeping me humble still makes me smile. He knew intuitively that this also meant helping me to laugh. It's a lesson I try to retain.

5. Wonder. One of the sorriest aspects of Aidan's story is that he was so wrapped up in coordinating the details of the catechumenate, he missed its highest moment of celebration.

"One who can no longer pause to wonder and stand rapt in awe is as good as dead."   — ALBERT EINSTEIN

My own experience was just the opposite. In my first position as a parish catechetical leader, I was responsible for directing and coordinating the RCIA. At the time I didn't even know what the initials stood for. I was in graduate school and decided to document my first year as a learning experience. I then walked the journey with the catechumens, candidates, sponsors, and spouses as a companion rather than a leader. At times, I felt as if I was watching from the back pew. Removing all expectations about my own "expertise" enabled me to truly marvel at the process. Each stage and rite became as meaningful for me as it did for the group. That experience remains in my memory as one of the most sacred of my life.

An artist once observed that if you know what you are looking for, you will never see what you do not expect to find. If we "know" how God will appear in our lives, we will never see or experience the Holy in unexpected times, events, people, or places. Rushing around and then trying to recapture an experience on videotape impedes being "rapt in awe." So, too, is trying to control everything through an obsession with perfectionism.

The caveat to Thomas Moore's observation about life becoming all function is that, in the process, we lose touch with beauty and art. Fundamentalism—spirituality that has lost its soul—is the result.

In Alice Walker's book *The Color Purple* (New York: Washington Square Press, 1982), there is a marvelous conversation about God between the two main characters. One of them reaches the conclusion that God loves admiration. "I think it pisses God off if you walk by the color purple in a field somewhere and don't notice it."

Think about it. What purple fields are you bypassing in order to get to the next "to-do"?

6. Be grateful. A few years ago, shortly before I moved to a new town and a new job, a group of friends gave me a gratitude journal. Each page contained inspirational quotes and space for recording a thought about gratitude for every day of the year. I embarked on the first Sunday of Advent. The year unfolded in painful and challenging ways. Thinking up a daily reason to be thankful was no small task.

"Sanctity has to do with gratitude. To be a saint is to be fueled by gratitude, nothing more and nothing less."

— RONALD ROLHEISER

In hindsight I see how much that exercise helped me through the year. I discovered what Sarah Ban Breathnach meant when she said, "Gratitude holds us together even when we're falling apart... While we cry ourselves to sleep, gratitude waits patiently to console and reassure us; there is a landscape larger than the one we can see."

Gratitude helps us to stop focusing on what's lacking in our lives and to attend to the grace that surrounds us. The story of the one leper out of ten (Luke 17:11–19) who returns to thank Jesus for his healing illustrates this nicely. Recognizing and expressing his gratefulness may have been the most redemptive aspect of the miracle, the returning leper's true healing.

We live in a culture that reveres the rights of the individual. Taken to its extreme this fosters an attitude of individual desires taking precedence over anyone else's. It makes the cultivation of gratitude an even greater challenge. Gratitude is intricately connected to wonder. If we are unable to wonder, to be in awe of life, it will be hard to be sincerely grateful for what surrounds us. What we need is a simple awareness of what we have today. Once we embrace the sacred in the ordinary, we appreciate each day as a gift from God.

7. Embrace mystery. It's been ten years since the terrorist attacks on the World Trade Center in New York and the Pentagon in Washington, D.C. Emotions over that terrible day are still raw. In the intervening years, other terrorist attacks have taken lives across the world, and devastating natural disasters have decimated communities in New Orleans, Haiti, Indonesia, and Japan, to name a few. Over and over again, people form the question about such horrific destructiveness—"How can this be?" It makes the efforts to minister to "colossal human brokenness" even more staggering. The gentle voice of the poet reminds us of the mysterious power of human touch, one-to-one, that keeps us from living in vain.

> *If I can ease one life the aching, or cool one pain,*
> *Or help one fainting robin unto his nest again,*
> *I shall not live in vain.*   — EMILY DICKINSON

We all experience adversity in our lives—through our work, and in our families, churches, and communities. How do we live graciously with suffering? How do we refrain from brushing it off or denying it? How do we keep from turning into cynics or losing hope? We often don't have time to reflect, let alone to recognize and mourn the losses we have experienced. Rachel Naomi Remen is a physician who has devoted the past several years of her life to working with care-givers. She notes how they eventually burn out, not because they don't care, but because they don't give themselves time to grieve the losses they experience in their work.

We also live with ambiguity. The older I get, the more I appreciate the stock response given to me as a child when I raised unanswerable questions about God. "It's a mystery," my teacher would say. I knew to go no further.

Wisdom figures rarely try to give their disciples answers; instead, they draw them into the questions themselves. As Thomas Moore says, "Care of the soul is not solving the puzzle of life; quite the opposite, it is an appreciation of the paradoxical mysteries that blend light and darkness into the grandeur of what human life and culture can be."

Our culture has a low level of tolerance for ambiguity and mystery. We want the "facts" and explanations. All sorts of products and entertainment are devised to steer us away from what is uncomfortable. One of our favorite devices is distraction. In *Ordinary Time: Cycles in Marriage, Faith, and Renewal* (Boston: Beacon Press, 1994), writer Nancy Mairs describes how she was encouraged to deal with the onslaught of multiple sclerosis by keeping busy. She was repelled by the idea that comfort came from distraction rather than contemplation and that, in order to maintain a cheerful attitude, one had to surrender the deepest parts of their lives. "It leads, oddly, to more self-pity than I care to feel, since one is bound to feel sorry for oneself if one believes one's circumstances too ghastly to bear scrutiny. The life left after such censoring seems to me crippled and contained."

The alternative, she suggests, is to go "all out" with whatever you have been handed and to think about it like mad. It's not a process of morbidity, but one of deep reflection based on the premise that what we deny knowing can hurt us.

8. Forgive. A woman I'll call Charlene once came to see me in order to discuss the struggles she was having with her ex-husband. He was a continual source of disruption in her life and in the lives of her children, and her anger toward him was escalating. "I want to let go of the power these attitudes have over me," she said. It was an exquisite example of a perfect confession. Charlene recognized her feelings as being her own and didn't project them onto someone else. She acknowledged the negative impact they were having on her life, and she wanted to let them go. Ultimately, she wanted to forgive this man and move on with her life.

> *"Forgiveness is the name of love practiced among people who love poorly."*   — HENRI NOUWEN

In the words of Marjorie J. Thompson, in her article, "Moving Toward Forgiveness" (*Weavings*, Vol. VII, no. 2): "To forgive is to make a conscious choice to release the person who has wounded us from the sentence of judgment, however justified that judgment may be." It is in this context that we can speak of forgetting. Charlene's wounds will never be completely forgotten—especially with her ex still in the picture—but their power over her was broken.

Forgiveness is a process that doesn't come cheaply or easily. As mentioned in Chapter 9, ministers may hold collective hurts that outweigh those of the people in their care. Working in an institution based on love sets our expectations high. We, too, need to relinquish the power those hurts have to bind us, to make us cynical and angry, to prevent us from embracing others in compassion and empathy.

Henri Nouwen once observed that if we don't first see ourselves as cherished and beloved by God, we will never be able to let go of past hurts. We will never be able to accept that, unlike God, other people can only love us imperfectly. Part of a daily spiritual regimen is to reflect upon the love God has for us as we also think about the hurts and fears that constrain us. It nurtures in us a forgiving and expansive heart.

9. Rest. Barbara Radtke's ministry students eventually came up with some advice for each other. Part of it advocated the setting of boundaries. This is a great antidote to overload and is a critical first step in learning to rest.

In her work with corporate clients, time management consultant Ann McGee-Cooper advocates the use of "joy breaks" throughout the day. These are short (three to five minutes) intervals for the purpose of having fun and decompressing. What she encounters in her work with people around the country is that many of them can't think of anything fun that takes less than thirty minutes. This creates a condition of being "joy-starved."

Many of us have ambivalent feelings about the idea of rest. We know we need it—indeed, we promote it in the lives of others—but feel guilty about doing "nothing." Even though God rested in the process of creating the world, we may feel our work is too important to do the same.

Jesus went off on a regular basis to hillsides and mountaintops to pray, but for many of us the idea of taking a day or an afternoon off for retreat is unthinkable. In the end, this does infinitely more harm than good. We need to place ourselves regularly in the life-giving Spirit of God. We need the Sabbath time of prayer. We have to rest in order to be authentic.

"Nearly every plant has a period of dormancy that is necessary to its further growth. And so, I suspect, do most human beings."
— KALEEL JAMISON

Part of the problem of finding rest is the tendency towards "monkey mind"—an incessant habit of picking at ourselves. We

Small pleasures that care for your soul

Here are twenty-five "five-minute ways" to refresh yourself:

1. Arrange a bouquet of flowers.

2. Savor a cup of hot chocolate.

3. Light a scented candle.

4. Read from a book of cartoons.

5. Eat a candy bar—slowly.

6. Walk around the block and look for the color purple.

7. Visit a Kindergarten class.

8. Write a thank-you note.

9. Listen to a favorite song.

10. Play a single hand of solitaire.

11. Log onto an inspirational website.

12. Write in your journal.

13. Pet a dog.

14. Dance around your office (door open or closed—your option).

15. Look at a photo of someone you love.

16. Send an email to a friend.

17. Compliment a coworker.

18. Read a magazine article that has nothing to do with your job.

19. Open your window and smell the fresh air.

20. Visit the church.

21. Drink a glass of cold water.

22. Compose a poem.

23. Practice a yoga exercise.

24. Read a children's story.

25. Offer a prayer for someone you love.

worry about what we do and how others perceive us. We fear judgment and criticism. Even though we know better, we think we need to be perfect. As Rachel Naomi Remen says: "To seek approval is to have no resting place, no sanctuary...It makes us uncertain of who we are and of our true value." This rings true for the approval we have for ourselves as well as what we offer to others. Approval is unreliable because it can be withdrawn at any time. No wonder its pursuit leaves us perpetually fatigued.

To find rest is to allow ourselves to release all of our struggles, our anxieties, our hurts, fears, and aspirations and to sink deeply into God's gracious care. Is there any better way to do this than through prayer?

10. Pray. Every part of this plan comes down to this: in order to care for ourselves as ministers, as believers, as human beings, we must pray.

This is such an obvious point, and yet church ministers are notorious for neglecting this part of their lives.

"The only one who prays well is the one who prays often."

— RICHARD ROHR

In Hebrew, the word "mercy" is derived from the same root word as "womb." Prayer allows us to rest in mercy by sinking into the still and silent waters of God's womb.

The rhythms of prayer that the Church has embraced for centuries are ones that have been adapted by various peoples for various circumstances. As pastoral ministers who live in the midst of a modern world, surely we can find creative ways to weave prayer into the days and seasons of our lives. Without it the fabric of our lives and our work frays and disintegrates.

The healthy parish minister

The only way things will be different for Aidan next year is if he takes responsibility for his own life. There are lots of other adjectives that can be used to describe the thousands of pastoral ministers who already know and embrace this fact. Enthusiastic, serene, energetic, hopeful, trusting, encouraging, creative, kind, and joyful are high on the list.

"A tree cannot stand in the storm without its roots embedded in the depths of the earth. We cannot stand in the storms of ministry without resting our roots deep in the healing silences of God." — RON FARR

I have been blessed in knowing many such pastoral ministers. They are the ones who have taught me the importance of coming to the well often for renewal and refreshment. They are the ones who carry the water of love and compassion to others. They are the ones who have taught me what I really need to know about parish ministry.

"What I DO know about parish ministry."

It is usually the simplest words that have the deepest meaning. One day when I was feeling particularly frazzled and frustrated, my friend, the late Bishop Michael Kenny, taught me the nightly prayer of Pope John XXIII. It says in nine words what I have been trying to say in a whole book. It is what I really do know about parish ministry.

"Lord, God, it's your Church. I'm going to bed."

Your thoughts

Now it's your turn to write down what you really do know:

▶ What I know about parish ministry.

▶ What I wish I knew about parish ministry and how I'm going to find out.

Bibliography

I have found these books to be particularly helpful.

Bausch, William J. *The Total Parish Manual.* Mystic, CT: Twenty-Third Publications, 1994.

Bennett-Goleman, Tara. *Emotional Alchemy: How the Mind Can Heal the Heart.* New York: Harmony Books, 2001.

Canfield, Jack and Jacqueline Miller. *Heart at Work.* New York: McGraw Hill, 1996.

Clifton, Donald O., and Paula Nelson. *Soar with Your Strengths.* New York: Delacorte Press, 1992.

De Pree, Max. *Leadership Is an Art.* New York: Dell Publishing, 1989.

De Pree, Max. *Leadership Jazz.* New York: Dell Publishing, 1992.

Gleick, James. *Faster: The Acceleration of Just About Everything.* New York: Pantheon Books, 1999.

Hater, Robert J. *New Vision, New Directions: Implementing the Catechism of the Catholic Church.* Allen, TX: Thomas More, 1994.

Hays, Edward. *Prayers for the Domestic Church.* Easton, KS: Forest of Peace, Inc., 1979.

Jamison, Kaleel. *The Nibble Theory and the Kernel of Power.* Mahwah, NJ: Paulist Press, 1984.

Keating, Charles J. *The Leadership Book.* Mahwah, NJ: Paulist Press, 1994.

Mairs, Nancy. *Ordinary Time: Cycles in Marriage, Faith, and Renewal.* Boston: Beacon Press, 1994.

McGee-Cooper, Ann. *Time Management for Unmanageable People.* New York: Bantam Books, 1994.

Moore, Thomas. *Care of the Soul: A Guide for Cultivating Depth and Sacredness in Everyday Life.* New York: HarperCollins, 1992.

Morrison, Emily Kittle. *Leadership Skills: Developing Volunteers for Organizational Success.* Tucson: Fisher Books, 1994.

Remen, Rachel Naomi. *Kitchen Table Wisdom: Stories That Heal.* New York: Riverhead Books, 1996.

Remen, Rachel Naomi. *My Grandfather's Blessings.* New York: Riverhead Books, 2000.

Rolheiser, Ronald. *The Holy Longing.* New York: Doubleday, 1999.

Sofield, Loughlan, Rosine Hammett, and Carroll Juliano. *Building Community.* Notre Dame, IN: Ave Maria Press, 1998.

Sofield, Loughlan and Carroll Juliano. *Collaboration: Uniting Our Gifts in Ministry.* Notre Dame, IN: Ave Maria Press, 2000.

Swain, Bernard. *Liberating Leadership: Practical Styles for Pastoral Ministry.* San Francisco: Harper and Row, Publishers, 1986.

Tannen, Deborah. *Talking from 9 to 5: Women and Men in the Workplace—Language, Sex, and Power.* New York: Avon Books, 1994.

Tannen, Deborah. *You Just Don't Understand.* New York: Ballantine Books, 1990.

Telushkin, Joseph. *Words That Hurt, Words That Heal.* New York: William Morrow and Company, 1996.

Tickle, Phyllis A. *Re-Discovering the Sacred.* New York: Crossroad Publishing Company, 1995.

Walker, Alice. *The Color Purple.* New York: Washington Square Press, 1982.

Weber, Christopher. *Jesus-Style Recruiting.* Alpharetta, GA: Visual Dynamics Publishing, 2011.